INVASIVE SPECIES

By Lisa J. Amstutz

ECOLOGICAL **DISASTERS**

Content Consultant
Art Gover
Research Support Associate
Department of Plant Science
Penn State College of Agricultural Sciences

Essential Library

An Imprint of Abdo Publishing | abdopublishing.com

abdopublishing.com

Published by Abdo Publishing, a division of ABDO, PO Box 398166, Minneapolis, Minnesota 55439. Copyright © 2018 by Abdo Consulting Group, Inc. International copyrights reserved in all countries. No part of this book may be reproduced in any form without written permission from the publisher. Essential Library™ is a trademark and logo of Abdo Publishing.

Printed in the United States of America, North Mankato, Minnesota
042017
092017

THIS BOOK CONTAINS
RECYCLED MATERIALS

Cover Photo: iStockphoto
Interior Photos: Auscape/Universal Images Group/Getty Images, 4–5, 99 (top right); Mark Higgins/Shutterstock Images, 6; Deposit Photos/Glow Images, 9; Shutterstock Images, 10, 44; Thomas Peter/Reuters/Newscom, 12; iStockphoto, 14, 16, 26, 34–35, 39, 40–41, 42, 47, 54, 62, 90–91, 98 (top left); 99 (right); Heiko Kiera/Shutterstock Images, 20–21; John Carnemolla/iStockphoto, 22, 99 (top left); Jeff Caughey/iStockphoto, 23; Nicola Margaret/iStockphoto, 24, 98 (right); Chris Watson/Shutterstock Images, 30; Francesco Tomasinelli & Emanuele Biggi/Science Source, 33; George Clerk/iStockphoto, 36; Red Line Editorial, 48, 76; Toby Talbot/AP Images, 52; Cliff Jette/The Gazette/AP Images, 53; Agence Nature/NHPA/Photoshot/Newscom, 57; Antoni Halim/iStockphoto, 59; John Flesher/AP Images, 63; Joe Raedle/Getty Images News/Getty Images, 64; Usda/Zuma Press/Newscom, 68–69; Science Source, 70; Steve Bittner/Cumberland Times-News/AP Images, 73; Matt Rourke/AP Images, 74–75; B.A.E. Inc/Alamy, 77; Craig Ruttle/AP Images, 78; Dolores Ochoa/AP Images, 80; Scott Takushi/Pioneer Press/AP Images, 82; Peter Titmuss/Alamy, 85; Anthony Souffle/Zuma Press/Newscom, 87; Mark Moffett/Minden Pictures/Newscom, 88; John Badman/The Telegraph/AP Images, 92–93; Bill O'Leary/The Washington Post/Getty Images, 94

Editor: Marie Pearson
Series Designer: Laura Polzin

Publisher's Cataloging-in-Publication Data

Names: Amstutz, Lisa J., author.
Title: Invasive species / by Lisa J. Amstutz.
Description: Minneapolis, MN : Abdo Publishing, 2018. | Series: Ecological
    disasters | Includes bibliographical references and index.
Identifiers: LCCN 2016962234 | ISBN 9781532110245 (lib. bdg.) |
    ISBN 9781680788099 (ebook)
Subjects: LCSH: Introduced organisms--Juvenile literature. | Biological invasions-
    -Juvenile literature. | Environmental degradation--Juvenile literature. |
    Ecological disturbances--Juvenile literature.
Classification: DDC 577--dc23
LC record available at http://lccn.loc.gov/2016962234

CONTENTS

ONE

A PLAGUE OF . . .

More than a century ago, a plague was unleashed on Australia. Hungry animals tore up the soil, chomped vegetation to the ground, and caused great harm to the ecosystem. Even fences could not stop the onslaught. What creature was causing so much trouble? European rabbits.

The first rabbits arrived in Australia in 1788 with the First Fleet, a group of convicts and sailors sent from Europe to settle in Australia.[1] Then, in 1859, the Victorian Acclimatisation Society brought 24 more rabbits to Australia to provide game for hunters and remind the settlers of

Rabbits' burrows have damaged land in Australia.

The Australian government built the world's longest fence to try to keep rabbits and dingoes from spreading. It is 3,488 miles (5,614 km) long.

home. The rabbits quickly spread. They have few predators in Australia, and they reproduce quickly. By the 1920s, there were approximately 10 billion bunnies in Australia.[2] The rabbits ate so much vegetation that native species such as wallabies and rat kangaroos did not have enough food. So the bunny battle began.

In 1907, the government tried building three long fences to keep rabbits from spreading to other parts of the country. But it was too late. The bunnies had already moved in. Later, cats and foxes were introduced to eat the rabbits. They ate some rabbits, but they ate native species too, causing even more stress to these species.

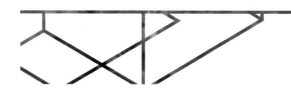

ARE INVASIVE SPECIES BAD?

Invasive species are not invasive everywhere. In their native habitats, they usually do not cause problems and may not even be very common. Their natural predators, competitors, parasites, and diseases keep them in check. Invasive species only become destructive when they arrive in a new place, away from these checks and balances.

In 1950, scientists hit on a method of biocontrol, the use of organisms to control pests. They introduced a rabbit virus that causes a disease called myxomatosis. The disease killed up to 99 percent of the rabbits in some areas.[3] However, it is spread by mosquitoes, which need water to reproduce. So the virus was not very effective in areas with a dry climate. Over time, the virus weakened, and some rabbits became resistant to it. It started to kill fewer and fewer rabbits. The rabbit population increased once again.

One female rabbit can have up to 30 babies per year.

PREVENTION IS THE BEST CURE

Benjamin Franklin once said, "An ounce of prevention is worth a pound of cure."[4] This wise saying certainly applies to invasive species: it is much easier to keep them out than to remove them once they've spread. It's also much less expensive. One of the best ways to prevent invasions is by teaching gardeners, pet owners, outdoor enthusiasts, and others about ways to keep invasive species from spreading. Stronger laws can also keep these species from being transported across state lines or from one country to another.

In 1995, a virus that causes rabbit calicivirus disease (RCD) escaped a research laboratory on an island near Australia when flies picked it up and carried it to the mainland. The virus spread quickly, and the population of rabbits crashed again. Recently, some endangered small animals have begun to recover thanks to the rabbit decline. But only time will tell if this will be a permanent solution. Some rabbit populations are already showing signs of resistance to the virus. Scientists are studying new, deadlier strains of the virus for use in the future. Meanwhile, the government continues to fight the bunny invasion using poisons, traps, fences, and biocontrols.

WHAT ARE INVASIVE SPECIES?

The European rabbit is an example of an invasive species—a species that arrives in a new area and causes harm. Invasive species can be plants, animals, fungi, or bacteria. They may harm the environment, other plants or animals, or human health. Next to habitat loss, they are considered the greatest threat to biodiversity in the world.

Approximately 1.4 trillion dollars are spent globally each year to control invasive species and repair the damage they cause.[5]

Not every exotic, or nonnative, species is invasive. Many, such as farm animals and crop plants, are useful to humans. People in the United States rely on exotic species such as cattle, chickens, wheat, rice, and potatoes for food. Others are

A female rabbit may have one litter every month.

used in landscaping or kept as pets. Approximately 50,000 exotic species can be found in the United States, and of these, approximately 4,300 are considered invasive.[6] This number is so high because Hawaii has many invasive species. Scientists estimate that globally approximately 10 percent of species introduced to a new area will survive and reproduce, and only approximately 10 percent of those will become invasive.[7]

SPECIES SPOTLIGHT: THE NILE PERCH

The Nile perch was introduced to Lake Victoria in Africa in 1962 for commercial fishing. This large fish is native to the Ethiopian region. It quickly began to dominate the ecosystem in Lake Victoria, causing hundreds of native fish species to go extinct.[8] It is a voracious predator and also carries parasites that can spread disease to other fish. The perch changed the ecosystem in other ways, as well. A large fishing industry quickly sprang up on the banks of Lake Victoria, displacing local people who traditionally fished in the lake. This affected both the economy and the environment of the area.

It usually takes years—sometimes even centuries—before an exotic species becomes a problem. The speed with which this happens depends on how fast the population can grow. Species that produce many young in a short period of time can multiply much more quickly than those that reproduce more slowly. Thus, fast reproducers, such as rabbits, are much more likely to become invasive than slow reproducers, such as elephants.

It's hard to pinpoint exactly what makes an organism become invasive. Scientists have proposed several different explanations. One of these is known as the enemy-release hypothesis. This hypothesis is based on the idea that in an ecosystem, nature has evolved to keep itself in balance. Predators, diseases, and competitors keep any one species from multiplying too quickly and taking over. However, when a species moves to a new ecosystem, it may not face such challenges. With nothing to impede its growth, it can quickly spread and outcompete native species for food and habitat. It disrupts the balance of the food web that is already in place, harming the native plants and animals that live there.

However, some invasive species do face predation and disease in their new habitats. And there must be some reason why only a small percentage of introduced species become invasive. The answer lies in the concept of fitness. Fitness is the ability of an organism to maintain or increase its numbers in the next generation. This ability depends on how well suited an organism is to its environment: whether it is good at finding resources, defending itself against predators and diseases, surviving the climate conditions, and so on. The fittest organism in an environment is best able to pass on its genes. Whatever the reason, invasive species are simply more fit than their native competitors.

Introduced species are most likely to become invasive in habitats that are already disturbed. For instance, the Nile perch's introduction is blamed for causing approximately 200 native fish species to go extinct in Lake Victoria.[9] However, the populations of these species had already been shrinking from overfishing, pollution, erosion, and excess nutrients. They were not well adapted to these changing conditions. The more-adaptable perch may have simply finished them off.

NATURAL INVADERS

In 1883, a massive volcanic eruption obliterated all life on Krakatoa, an island near Java and Sumatra in the Indian Ocean. But it didn't take long for plants and animals to recolonize the island. Spiders were the first animals to arrive, likely carried on the wind. Soon, grasses and other plants sprouted from seeds carried by the wind or in the droppings of passing birds. Today, birds nest and sing in the lush rain forest on Krakatoa.

Feral cats can quickly take over islands, as they have done on Aoshima Island in Japan.

THE RIPPLE EFFECT

In any ecosystem, there is a delicate balance of nature. Just like pulling a single thread can unravel a whole sweater, introducing a new organism can have drastic and complex effects on all the other organisms in an ecosystem.

Such a ripple effect, also called a trophic cascade, took place on Macquarie Island near Australia after several different species were introduced. First, rats and mice arrived accidentally on ships. When they became a problem, sailors brought cats to the island to control the rodents. In 1878, seal hunters introduced rabbits to the island to provide a food source for their long journeys. Although some of the rabbits were eaten by cats, they still devastated the native vegetation. So in 1968, scientists introduced the rabbit myxoma virus to the island to control the rabbits. Slowly, the vegetation began to grow back. But now the cats had nothing to eat. They started eating birds instead.

In 1985, scientists started a program to remove the cats. By 2000, the cats were gone. But with no cats to keep it in check, the rabbit population skyrocketed. Again they began to destroy the vegetation.

In some cases, the changes brought about by an invasive species can even change the environment itself. For instance, a South American tree known as the velvet tree has invaded mountainous areas of Hawaii. It grows so thickly that it has almost completely replaced the native understory in some areas. Its shallow root system does not hold the soil in place as securely as the species it replaces. This has led to numerous landslides on the steep mountain slopes.

Cheatgrass quickly grows large root systems that often use up groundwater before native plant seedlings grow their own root systems.

An annual grass called cheatgrass encourages wildfires in the areas it invades. Before cheatgrass invaded Utah's Great Basin, fires came along every 60 to 110 years. Today, they happen every 3 to 5 years.[10] While the native vegetation tends to grow in small clumps, highly flammable cheatgrass fills in the spaces, allowing fire to spread rapidly. In addition, cheatgrass seeds spring up quickly after a fire, while native plants may be killed off. Animals such as the sage grouse and pygmy rabbit rely on these native plants for food and habitat, so their populations suffer when cheatgrass takes over.

People can knowingly or unknowingly transport seeds or insects to other countries with their luggage. The insects or plants may become invasive.

TWO

HITCHHIKERS AND ESCAPEES

Living things have always moved around. Seeds hitch rides in animal fur or float in ocean currents. Birds and insects get carried off course by air currents. Humans carry domesticated plants and animals with them as they colonize new areas. But movement happens at a much faster rate these days, thanks to technology. A hundred years ago, humans traveled at the pace of a horse or sailing ship. Today, people speed around the world in planes and cars. Often, travelers carry potentially invasive species with them.

Native Americans had no immunity to smallpox when it arrived with Europeans. In 1837, smallpox killed nine out of every ten Mandans, including their chief and his family.

Until recently, most invasive species moved from Europe and Asia to North America and New Zealand and other islands. They were carried either accidentally or on purpose by explorers and settlers. Human diseases such as smallpox and weeds such as Canada thistle were some of the first to arrive. Other early invaders included animals closely associated with humans, such as rats, cockroaches, lice, and bedbugs. Most organisms could not survive the months-long journey to the New World unless they lived on humans or animals, in stored grains, or in soil carried as ballast. Thus, most early invaders were of these hardy types.

In the late 1800s, steamships began to cross the ocean at much faster speeds than the old sailing ships, and the rate of invasion increased dramatically. By the early 1900s, the US government had begun to make laws against importing certain types of exotic species, but the number of invasive species continued to climb. In recent decades, increasing trade with Asia has brought even more invasive species to North America.

ACCLIMATIZATION SOCIETIES

In the last half of the 1800s, a new fad swept across the United States, Canada, Europe, New Zealand, and Australia. People formed clubs called acclimatization societies with the goal of introducing animals that seemed useful or reminded them of home. They imported a wide variety of species, some of which quickly became invasive. One of these was the house or English sparrow, which was brought to the United States in the 1850s. A less successful scheme involved introducing camels to the American Southwest.

INVITED GUESTS

Some invasive species were introduced on purpose. As ecologist Dr. Daniel Simberloff wrote, "People are never happy with the species they have."[1] Throughout history, people

MORE PLANTS, PLEASE!

Until the 1900s, the effects of adding exotic species to the landscape were poorly understood. The US government actually encouraged people to import useful plants. Thomas Jefferson once wrote that "the greatest service which can be rendered any country is to add an useful plant to it's [sic] culture."[2] The US Office of Plant Introduction introduced approximately 200,000 different plants to the country from 1887 to the early 1900s.[3] But by the 1900s, problems were becoming evident. The government reversed its position and began introducing laws to keep new plants out.

have transported plants and animals around the world for use as food or medicine. For instance, the common dandelion, the bane of many a homeowner's existence, was brought to the United States by settlers from Europe. They planted it in their gardens to use as food and medicine. The plant spreads easily, especially in disturbed areas such as farmland, and today it is considered a weed. Other plants have been imported for landscaping, as animal feed, or simply because they reminded someone of home.

Another reason species are introduced is to control other pests. This can be a good solution to a pesky problem. But if it is not done carefully, the new species may turn out to be an even bigger problem than the original pest.

The harlequin ladybird, also known as the Asian ladybird beetle or Asian ladybug, is one such invader. It was brought to the United States from Asia to kill aphids and other pest insects. That turned out to be a bad idea, as the introduced beetles quickly became pests themselves. They are larger and hungrier than their native cousins and outcompete them for food. They will even eat other ladybugs' eggs and larvae. In addition, harlequin ladybirds can carry a fungal virus that does not affect them but kills native ladybugs.

A harlequin ladybird beetle can eat more than 5,300 aphids in its lifetime.[4]

Harlequin ladybirds cause particular problems for winemakers. The beetles cluster in bunches of grapes and are crushed along with them. This makes the wine made with those grapes taste and smell bad. They also have an annoying tendency to cluster in people's homes. Harlequin ladybirds have now spread through much of Europe and several countries in South America and Africa. Native ladybugs are in serious decline in many of these areas.

PETS ON THE LOOSE

Pets play an important role in many people's lives. Unfortunately, pets can easily become pests if not properly contained. Pet owners sometimes release their pets into the wild if the pets grow too big or they no longer want them. Pets sometimes escape their cages, as well.

Few people want a 23-foot (7 m), 200-pound (90 kg) snake in their house. That's the size of a full-grown Burmese python.[5] Until the government banned the importation and interstate sale or transport of these snakes in 2012, they were frequently brought into the United States from Southeast Asia and sold as pets. When they became too big to care for, many owners simply released them.

The pet trade is responsible for more than 80 percent of the exotic reptile and amphibian species found in Florida.[6]

MICROBES ON THE MOVE

Plants and animals are the most publicized invasive species, but some microbes can be considered invasive as well. For example, the smallpox germs brought to North America by European explorers killed thousands of Native Americans. Many times, these microbes are carried on other invasive species; for example, rodents carried fleas that carried the bacteria that caused the bubonic plague in Europe. Asian tiger mosquito eggs in used tires imported from Asia were responsible for introducing dog heartworm disease to the United States.

Today, at least 10,000 pythons are terrorizing the Florida Everglades.[7] They threaten humans, eat native animals, and destroy ecosystems. Pythons wrap their muscular bodies around their prey and squeeze it to death. They feed on more than 20 different types of animals in the Everglades and have wiped out 99 percent of the deer, raccoon, marsh rabbits, opossums, and bobcats in some areas.[8] A python can even kill an alligator or panther. Burmese pythons can breed for more than 20 years, laying up to 100 eggs per year.[9] Because of the swampy terrain in the Everglades, it is nearly impossible for authorities to find and eliminate them.

Wild animals aren't the only pets that become destructive when released. Domestic animals can cause trouble as well. A cute little kitten can turn into a terror when it becomes feral. Feral animals are those that are normally domesticated, like cats

Burmese pythons are the largest python species invading the Everglades.

21

PIGS ON THE LOOSE

Considered one of the world's 100 worst invaders, feral pigs are found on every continent but Antarctica and on many islands as well.[14] Brought by early seafarers as food, the pigs either escaped or were set free, and they quickly multiplied. Pigs feed on vegetation and small animals, and they can damage crops, forests, and other plant communities by trampling and rooting for food. They also carry diseases that can pass to humans and other animals.

or pigs, but have returned to living in the wild. House cats were first domesticated approximately 3,000 years ago. Since that time, humans have carried them to almost every part of the world. In the United States alone, 100 million feral and outdoor cats kill more than one billion wild birds every year.[10] Feral cats have particularly affected bird populations on islands.

HITCHING A RIDE

Organisms are sometimes carried to new places accidentally. Ships have been responsible for the spread of many species. For example, Norway rats from Europe hitched rides to North America, Australia, and many islands around the world in ship holds. Organisms can also be carried in ballast water. Water is taken in at one port and released at the next. Plants, small fish, crabs, clams, and other organisms are sucked into the tanks along with the water and dumped out at the next port. Multiply this by more than 45,000 cargo ships carrying approximately 12 billion tons of ballast water per year, and it adds up to a huge problem.[11] Scientists estimate that 10,000 species are transported globally in ballast water every day.[12]

Female Norway rats can produce up to seven litters per year of up to 14 young each.[15]

In the 1980s, the zebra mussel traveled from Europe to the Great Lakes in North America, most likely in ship ballast. Each dime-sized mussel lays up to 500,000 eggs per year.[13]

Zebra mussels attach themselves to solid surfaces, including boats. If the boat is transported to another lake, the mussels can quickly invade that lake, too.

With no natural predators in the Great Lakes, it grows thickly, forming clusters of up to 70,000 individuals per 10.8 square feet (1 sq m) in places.[16] The zebra mussel has spread throughout the Great Lakes and several surrounding rivers, clogging pipes and waterways.

As it filters water, the zebra mussel feeds on phytoplankton. It competes for food with native mussels, and at times grows so thickly on top of them that it chokes them out. Zebra mussels cause billions of dollars of damage each year in the Great Lakes region.

Goats are generalists because they eat many kinds of foods. They even climb trees to feed on leaves.

Chapter
THREE

FUEL TO THE FIRE

When a plant or animal arrives in a new environment, it faces many challenges. It needs a habitat to live in and food to eat. It must avoid new dangers. Successful invaders tend to have several things in common. They are generalists rather than specialists, able to use various types of food and resources. They can also tolerate a broad temperature range and reproduce quickly. In short, they're flexible. But several factors can add fuel to the fire, making these exotic species even more likely to spread. These include climate change, the island effect, a lack of predators, and habitat destruction.

SPECIES SPOTLIGHT: WATER HYACINTH

The water hyacinth of Brazil has invaded waterways throughout the southern United States, Hawaii, and California. The plant's glossy leaves and showy lavender-blue flowers make it a popular aquarium plant, and its sale is still allowed in some states. It grows quickly, forming thick mats that choke off waterways. The plant cannot tolerate cold temperatures, but Earth's changing climate may allow it to expand its range northward.

CLIMATE CONCERNS

Growing amounts of carbon dioxide in the atmosphere are causing Earth's climate to change rapidly. Scientists warn that average temperatures may increase by approximately 9 degrees Fahrenheit (5°C) by 2100.[1] By 2050, up to 37 percent of species may be headed for extinction. As temperatures continue to change, invasive species will likely become an even bigger problem than they are today.

There are several ways this could happen. First, warming temperatures may make it easier for certain species to spread out of their native ranges. For instance, cold temperatures limit the range of the mountain pine beetle, which bores into and damages pine trees. However, as temperatures rise, the beetle is expanding its range into higher latitudes and altitudes. Second, the changing climate may cause additional stress to native species and ecosystems, making them weaker and more vulnerable to invasion by stronger competitors. Some species' ranges may shrink, making extinction more likely. Third, some species seem to tolerate high levels of carbon dioxide better than others do. This gives them an advantage in a changing climate. For example, an invasive aquatic plant called hydrilla grows faster when temperatures and carbon dioxide levels increase. Native to the Eastern Hemisphere, it spread to the southern and coastal United States through the aquarium trade. Scientists believe it may expand its range even farther as climate conditions continue to change. Lastly, the changing climate is increasing the number of disturbances such as wildfires and hurricanes, giving an advantage to species that thrive in disturbed areas.

THE ISLAND EFFECT

Twenty-five percent of the endangered species recognized by the US government live in Hawaii, one of many island habitats that have suffered great damage from invasive species.[2] The effect of invasive species seems to be magnified on islands; in fact, 75 percent of all recorded extinctions have taken place in island ecosystems because the species there are more vulnerable.[3]

There are several possible reasons for this. First, island ecosystems are usually smaller and less diverse than those on the mainland. This means that there are fewer species and fewer individuals of each species to begin with. Hawaii has roughly 2,500 introduced and 5,000 native insect species. The US mainland, by contrast, has about 3,000 introduced and 96,000 native insect species.[4] Thus, the impact of each new arrival on the mainland is much smaller.

Second, island species may have fewer defenses against enemies. If an island has no large predators, for example, the animals living there do not develop defenses against them.

WHY ARE SOME AREAS MORE PRONE TO INVASION?

Some ecosystems seem to be much more vulnerable to invasion than others. Few species have invaded the boreal forests of North America and Eurasia or the tropical forests of Africa, Asia, South America, and Australia. Extremely dry or cold environments, such as deserts and polar regions, suffer fewer invasions as well. Scientists are not sure if this is coincidence or if some kind of resistance is found in these places.

Additionally, animals on islands with no natural predators tend to be more passive than those in other areas. They may not respond as quickly to danger.

Perhaps the biggest problem, however, is that many islands have lost a large amount of natural habitat. This means that the remaining animals have smaller ranges and may not have any refuges. They are therefore more vulnerable to extinction when an invader comes along. On the island of Guam, many forest habitats were destroyed as US and Japanese forces waged war in the early 1940s. Some areas were cleared, and others were bombed or burned. Invasive tangantangan trees were then planted to keep the soil from eroding. Invasive animals such as Norway rats, feral cats, and green anoles moved in as well. The combination of these changes left forest-dwelling birds more vulnerable to extinction when the brown tree snake arrived on the scene.

OH, NUTS!

When the North American eastern gray squirrel arrived in the United Kingdom in 1876, it turned out to be better at finding nuts than the native red squirrels. Because it outcompetes them for food, it has caused a decline in red squirrel populations. The gray squirrels carry a disease called squirrel pox, which they are immune to but can pass to their British cousins. They also damage certain kinds of trees by stripping their bark in winter, leaving them vulnerable to disease.

LACK OF PREDATORS

Another factor that increases the impact of introduced species is a lack of natural predators to keep them in check. The cane toad is a prime example. Cane toads hopped onto the continent of Australia in 1935, when they were imported to feed on beetles that were damaging sugarcane crops. However, it soon became clear that the toads had little effect on the pests.

This might not have been a huge problem, except that the cane toad has few natural predators in Australia. Even animals that normally feed on toads cannot eat a cane toad, because when it is threatened, the cane toad makes a poison in glands on its shoulders. It can even squirt the poison a short distance. Any predator that tries to eat a cane toad or gets too close soon dies a painful death. Cane toad eggs are poisonous as well. Snakes are especially threatened by the cane toad because they come into contact with a large amount of toxin when swallowing the toads whole. Humans have also died from eating the toads or their eggs.

By 1950, cane toads had become a serious problem. Today there are billions of them in Australia.[5] Hand-removal methods are not terribly effective, since the toads lay up to 30,000 eggs at a time.[6] Scientists are working on a variety of ways to deal with the problem, including traps baited with cane toad eggs (the toads are cannibalistic) and viruses to interfere with the toads' growth.

HABITAT DESTRUCTION

Meeting a red imported fire ant is an experience that's hard to forget. These aggressive stinging ants were accidentally brought to Alabama from South America in the 1930s. Today,

Scientists are attempting to save the endangered northern quoll, a small marsupial, from cane toad poisoning by dropping sausages made from cane toad legs from helicopters. The sausages are laced with nausea-inducing chemicals that will possibly deter the kitten-sized quolls from eating cane toads in the future.

A black kite eats a cane toad. The toad's poison tends to be less deadly to birds than to reptiles and mammals.

they range from North Carolina to Texas. Attempts to get rid of the ants have been unsuccessful. Pesticides used in the 1950s killed other wild animals and livestock as well. Chemical baits killed the ants for a time, but they soon came back.

Fire ants seem to be advancing rapidly. Studies show that fire ants prefer disturbed areas, where native ant populations are already declining. In areas that the researchers mowed or plowed, fire ants moved in faster than their colonies could be removed.

Studies on plants reveal a similar pattern. Ecologists studying the Garry oak meadows of southwestern British Columbia in Canada found that the changes in this habitat are mostly due to human suppression of fires. Until recent decades, fires were started by lightning, and native peoples frequently burned the meadows. These fires removed grasses, shrubs, and young trees that could not tolerate fire. This kept fuel from accumulating, so most fires were not intense enough to kill the larger oaks, allowing smaller native plants to quickly resprout. Fires also kept invasive species from taking over. These conditions favored the oak meadow ecosystem. Since humans started putting out fires to prevent property damage, fires that do occur are much more intense and can kill the oak trees and native plants. The meadows are now dominated by invasive species. The new conditions favor the invaders.

Humans have disturbed a large portion of the habitats on Earth by clearing land for agriculture, housing, and industry and by putting pollutants into the air, water, and soil. Unfortunately, as Earth's population continues to grow, habitat destruction is likely to continue.

DEVELOPING DEFENSES

Given enough time, native species can evolve defenses against invaders. In areas where the red fire ant threatens fence lizards, for example, the lizards have developed longer legs and a tail-flicking behavior that helps them escape attacking ants. Fence lizards that do not have these adaptations cannot fight off the ants when they attack.

A FROGGY FUNGUS

In the early 1990s, scientists in California, Costa Rica, and Australia noticed something strange. Frogs and toads were dying, and no one knew why. They seemed to have a mild skin condition but otherwise looked healthy. The scientists found some strange single-celled organisms in the amphibians' tissues but didn't know what they were. Finally, in 1997, the organisms were identified as a type of chytrid fungus named *Batrachochytrium dendrobatidis*, or *Bd*.

This group of fungi had never been known to cause disease in vertebrates, and such a widespread amphibian disease had never been seen before. Nevertheless, all the evidence pointed to *Bd* as the culprit. The disease continued to spread, and today it is blamed for the decline or extinction of more than 200 species of amphibians.[7]

Many of these species were already in trouble. Not only is their habitat shrinking due to human activities, but these thin-skinned animals absorb oxygen and water through their skin. Pesticides and other pollutants in the water as well as changes in temperature or humidity can kill or weaken them, possibly making them more susceptible to *Bd*. Another possibility is that changes in the environment somehow favor the growth of the fungus. Whatever the cause of the decline in frogs and toads, it appears that *Bd* delivered the final blow. Two possible culprits in the spread of *Bd* are the African clawed frog and American bullfrog, invasive species that can carry the disease without getting sick.

Chapter FOUR

INVASIVE LAND ANIMALS

L and animals are some of the most noticeable invasive species. Because they tend to prefer disturbed habitats, they are often found in places where humans live. Most people encounter invasive species every day, from pigeons in the park to armadillos in the yard to ladybugs on the windshield.

European starlings damage crops across the United States.

MESMERIZING MURMURATIONS

Starlings often form huge flocks called murmurations. Thousands of birds blacken the sky as the swarm dips and swirls. The presence of a falcon or other predator often causes the flock to take flight. Rather than flying about in mass confusion, the birds quickly share information across the flock to move as a group. When one changes speed or direction, the whole flock responds. Scientists aren't entirely sure how the birds synchronize their movements so perfectly, but it appears that they coordinate them with their seven nearest neighbors in the flock.[4]

SPREAD OF THE STARLINGS

The year was 1890. In New York City's Central Park, a man named Eugene Schieffelin turned the latch on a large crate of European starlings. Gently, he lifted the lid and released the spotted, iridescent black birds—more than 120 in all.[1] Eugene smiled with satisfaction as the birds flew off. He was one step closer to his goal: stocking Central Park with every species of bird mentioned in Shakespeare's works.

Eugene got his wish—and then some. These aggressive birds made themselves right at home in the city and quickly spread. They ate almost anything and outcompeted native birds for food. Today, there are an estimated 200 million starlings in North America.[2] They cost US farmers more than $800 million a year in damages.[3] Flocks descend on fields and orchards and steal food from farm animals. They damage plants, eat fruits, and even pull out sprouting grain plants. In the city, starling droppings coat buildings and sidewalks and carry disease. Starlings take over native birds' nesting places.

It is difficult to kill starlings without killing other birds in the process. Traps may be used, but the birds are more commonly managed by other methods. Farmers are encouraged to clean up spilled grain and use bird-proof animal feeders. Recorded distress calls, lights, and noisemakers can be used to scare starlings away from crops.

Starlings are good mimics. They can learn up to 20 different birdcalls and can even imitate a telephone ring or car alarm.[7]

PIGEON POOP

The rock dove, or pigeon, is another invited guest that overstayed its welcome. It was brought to the United States in the 1600s as a food source. It quickly became a pest, however. Pigeons like to live near people, either near farmland or in cities. They eat garbage, seeds, and insects. They often get into stored food as well. Pigeons even cause problems for aircraft by flying into their engines.

But one of the biggest problems with pigeons is their poop. They produce a lot of it—an average of 25 pounds per bird per year, to be exact. Pigeon droppings cause $1.1 billion in damage to US cities every year by corroding buildings, cars, fire escapes, and monuments.[5] Worse yet, they can spread diseases such as salmonella.

ATTACK OF THE SWANS

It's hard to picture the tall, graceful mute swan as a pest, but its behavior is, at times, not so elegant. These decorative birds were brought from Europe to North America in the late 1800s to adorn parks and ponds. However, they have a large appetite for aquatic plants and can uproot 20 pounds of them per day.[6] Left unchecked, flocks of mute swans may harm native plant populations. This reduces the amount of food available for other waterfowl.

UNEXPECTED EFFECTS

The effects of invasive species are not always direct or predictable. When bald eagles started dying in Georgia, it took some detective work to figure out the cause: hydrilla. The eagles did not eat the plants directly; they ate water birds called coots that had eaten algae growing on the hydrilla mats. These algae contain a neurotoxin. When concentrated in an animal's body, it can be deadly.

Mute swans are very aggressive about protecting their territory. They chase away native birds such as loons, preventing them from nesting and sometimes even attacking and killing their young. They will even attack people in boats or on the shore. These large birds can cause serious injury, especially to small children.

SWAMP RATS RULE

The nutria, sometimes called a swamp rat, is a shaggy little rodent native to South America. Fur farmers brought it to the United States in 1899. But by the 1940s, people no longer wanted to buy nutria coats or hats. Unable to sell nutria pelts, some farmers released their animals into the wild. Other nutrias escaped during storms and floods.

Nutrias have now been found in at least 22 states.[8] They have also invaded parts of Canada, Europe, Asia, and East Africa. Not only do they destroy marshes and break down riverbanks, harming the habitat for animals such as muskrats, crabs, and young fish, but they also tear up the nests of birds and small animals. Nutrias can carry diseases and parasites, such as tuberculosis and tapeworms, that affect humans.

Nutrias have a big appetite for marsh grasses. They chew them down to the root with their big orange teeth, turning wetlands into big mudflats or open water habitat. They sometimes feed on crop plants such as wheat, oats, and peanuts as well. The animals reproduce quickly—females give birth to litters of up to 13 young and average more than two litters per year.[9]

Part of the nutria's success is due to the sorry state of many of the wetlands it colonizes. Pollutants from farms and factories, along with the damming of rivers and draining of wetlands, have damaged many native wetland areas. The nutria, however, seems to thrive in these mucky, polluted conditions.

One of the best ways to control nutrias is by trapping them. The state of Louisiana started a bounty program in 2002, paying trappers $5 per nutria tail.[10] The program has been a success, reducing the number of affected acres from a high of 102,585 (41,515 ha) in 1999 to just 6,008 (2,431 ha) in 2015.[11] The bounty program has encouraged entrepreneurs to find new uses for the animals, from barbecued meat to fur-lined miniskirts to nutria-tooth jewelry.

SPECIES SPOTLIGHT: INDIAN MONGOOSE
The introduction of the Indian mongoose seemed like a good idea at the time. The furry predators were brought to Hawaii, Fiji, the West Indies, Okinawa, and other islands to control rats and snakes. Unfortunately, they developed a taste for other species as well, and caused many mammals, birds, reptiles, and amphibians on these islands to become endangered or extinct.

REINDEER REMOVAL

On the island of South Georgia in the southern Atlantic Ocean, reindeer wreaked havoc for many years. Norwegian whalers introduced reindeer to the island in the early 1900s to use as a food supply on long whaling voyages. At first the herd was maintained with the

whalers' hunting. When the whaling operation shut down and the hunting ended, the reindeer population exploded. Far from the herd's normal Arctic range and unchecked by predators, its population grew to around 3,000. They overgrazed and trampled the vegetation, threatening king penguins and other native birds by damaging their nests and habitat.[12] In 2013 and 2014, a team of scientists and Sami reindeer herders from Norway rounded up and shot the reindeer. The meat was collected and sold. The following year, rats were eradicated from the island. Native birds and vegetation are already showing signs of recovery.

Nutria burrows can cause stream banks to erode.

GIANT AFRICAN SNAILS

For the past two centuries, giant African snails have been inching their way outward from their native East Africa. These huge snails can grow up to 8 inches (20 cm) long, feed on more than 500 different crops, and leave a gooey trail of slime behind.[13] Giant African snails can now be found on every continent except Antarctica.

How can a species that literally moves at a snail's pace spread so far, so fast? It had help from humans. The snails have been used as medicine, to decorate gardens, and as food. They have also been imported accidentally in shipments of plants or soil, or by tourists who thought the shells were empty.

The nine-banded armadillo was historically found in the southeastern United States, but recently it has been spotted as far north as Nebraska and Illinois.

ARMORED INVADERS

Nine-banded armadillos are a common sight in the southern United States. These tank-like mammals are covered in bony armored plates. Native to South America, armadillos migrated into Texas in the 1880s and have slowly moved eastward and northward. Human changes to the landscape and removal of large predators may have made it easier for the armadillos to spread. Not even rivers can stop their advance— the armadillos simply hold their breath and either walk across the bottom or swim. Armadillos can hold their breath for up to six minutes.[14]

Armadillos feed at night, digging for insects and other small animals with their sharp claws. This can be a positive thing when they eat grubs or fire ants. However, their burrows can also cause soil erosion and damage buildings, fields, and yards. In addition, armadillos sometimes eat the eggs of endangered sea turtles.

INVASION OF THE TEGU

An Argentine lizard is causing concern among scientists in central and southern Florida. The black-and-white tegu, which can grow to 4 feet (1.2 m) in length, is spreading quickly and poses a serious threat to Florida's wildlife.[15] Tegus feed on fruits, vegetables, small animals, and eggs, and may threaten endangered species, such as crocodiles, sea turtles, and ground-nesting birds. Several state agencies are working together to try to trap the lizards before they spread further.

A pet's fur can collect seeds called burs, transporting the burs as the animal travels with its owner.

Chapter
FIVE

HOW PLANTS MOVE AROUND

C onsidering that most of them are rooted to the ground, plants do a surprising amount of traveling. Much of this movement is by seeds; for example, coconut trees are found on many tropical islands because their seeds, coconuts, washed up on shore and sprouted. Dandelion seeds are carried by wind to far-off places, and burs containing seeds stick to animal fur. Some seeds even sprout after they've passed through the gut of a fruit-eating animal and been dropped with its feces.

Plants can move in other ways, too. Small plants such as duckweed may stick to the feet, feathers, or fur of aquatic animals. Birds also carry plants to use as nesting material, thus dispersing their seeds. But perhaps the most common way that plants move is by human transportation. People take plants to new areas for use as food, medicine, and animal feed, as well as for use in landscaping. They also carry them accidentally on vehicles, firewood, and clothing.

THE VINE THAT ATE THE SOUTH

It sounds like something from a horror movie—a vine that can grow 1 foot (0.3 m) per day and swallows up everything it comes across.[1] Visitors to the southeastern United States will understand why kudzu has been called "the vine that ate the South."[2] The vine smothers trees by draping itself over them so thickly that sunlight cannot reach them. Kudzu also competes with native plants for nutrients in the soil. Its weight can even collapse buildings and power lines.

Kudzu was brought to the United States from Asia in 1876 as an ornamental plant. People were encouraged to plant it; in fact, the government actually handed out 85 million kudzu seedlings and paid farmers $8 per acre to plant them in the 1930s and 1940s. The goal was to help prevent erosion.[3] Kudzu has pretty purple flowers and makes a good shade plant. It can be used for making baskets, paper, tea, jellies, and syrups. It has been used in herbal medicines to treat allergies, flu, snake

SWALLOWED BY VINES

If it is not removed, kudzu will completely engulf power lines, vehicles, and even buildings. The weight of the vines can cause these structures to collapse. Kudzu vines can grow to 98 feet (30 m) in length, with up to 30 vines sprouting from a single root crown.[4] They can cause power outages by collapsing poles or wires. It costs power companies in the southern United States an estimated $1.5 million per year to remove them.[5] Kudzu also causes problems for railroads. When trains drive over it, they grind it into a slippery mash that can cause the train to slip or even derail.

Kudzu can quickly overtake a forest.

and insect bites, and even hangovers. Kudzu also makes good animal feed for cows, goats, and sheep. But like many invasive species, kudzu has few natural enemies in the United States and thrives in disturbed areas. It began to spread widely. By 1972, it was considered a weed. Today, kudzu covers more than 7 million acres (2.8 million ha) in the South.[6] Controlling kudzu

Kudzu's underground growth is impressive, too. Its roots can weigh several hundred pounds and stretch up to 12 feet (3.6 m) in length.[7]

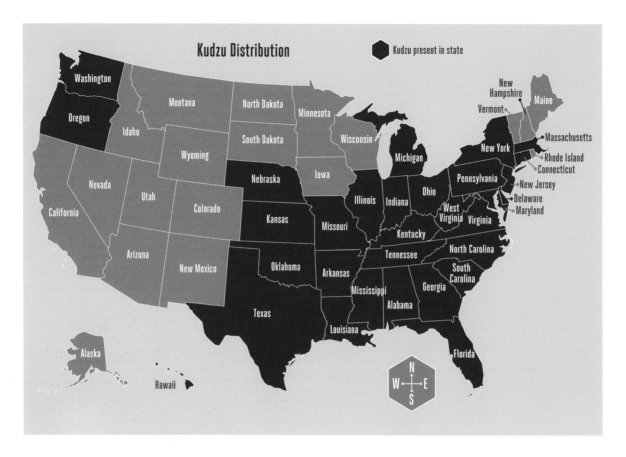

Kudzu has been found in 31 states.

is very difficult. It produces seeds, but it spreads mainly through runners, rhizomes, and new plants sprouting from nodes on the vines. Pieces carried by water, vehicles, or other machinery can easily take root and grow. Killing it is problematic. Mowing can be effective on a small scale but must be repeated for several years. Burning is also effective, but it kills other species along with the kudzu. Chemical weed killers, called herbicides, often damage other species, too, and must be applied for several years. One of the best methods for removing kudzu from a small area is by grazing animals, such as goats or pigs. Grazing for three to four years is usually effective at eliminating the weed.[8] However, it is difficult to do on a large scale. A fungal disease is being studied for possible use against kudzu as well.

THE PURPLE PLAGUE

A wetland filled with purple loosestrife looks beautiful. However, the effects of this invasive plant are not so lovely. Purple loosestrife came to the United States in the early 1800s from Europe for use as a garden plant. Free of the competitive pressures that kept it in check in its native range, this perennial plant has invaded wetlands along the East Coast, crowding out native plants. It grows especially well on disturbed surfaces and can easily take over an entire marsh. By 2000, it covered 16 million acres (6.5 million ha).[9] Today, it is found in every state but Florida and Hawaii. About $45 million per year is spent to control purple loosestrife and restore habitats it has damaged.

One reason loosestrife survives is that it is a generalist species and can live in many different environments as long as it has enough moisture. The plant can make temporary changes during its life cycle to adjust to its environment. For example, it may grow longer leaves to adjust to low-light conditions. This is called phenotypic plasticity, and it is one reason that purple loosestrife is such a successful invader.

BAT KILLERS

Over 6.7 million bats in North America have died since 2006 from an introduced fungus called bat white-nose syndrome.[10] This disease likely arrived on the clothing of a visitor from Europe. The disease is common there, but most European bats are resistant to it. It spreads quickly because bats groom each other and pack closely together in caves. To prevent the disease from spreading further, visitors to US caves are asked to disinfect their clothing before and after visiting.

TRIFFID WEED

An American plant known as triffid weed, paraffin bush, or bitter bush is threatening the survival of crocodiles on the other side of the world. Seeds of this invasive plant arrived in South Africa in packing material aboard a ship. It grows near Lake Saint Lucia, where threatened Nile crocodiles breed. The tall, bushy plant has taken over many of the sunny, sandy banks where the crocodiles nest. It shades the eggs, lowering the surrounding temperature by approximately 9 degrees Fahrenheit (5°C).[12] Because the sex of baby crocodiles is determined by the temperature of their eggs, only females hatch out in these areas. Without males to breed with, they cannot reproduce.

Another reason loosestrife is so successful is that it produces a vast number of seeds—a single plant can release as many as two to three million seeds per year.[11] The tiny seeds can be spread by wind or water. They can also be carried on boats, car tires, clothing, or the feathers or feet of birds. Loosestrife stems can put out new shoots that can detach and grow into more loosestrife plants.

While it provides nectar for some native bees and butterflies, purple loosestrife causes declines in other wildlife populations, such as that of the bog turtle. The plants grow so densely that the turtle cannot move around. It has also affected the black tern and marsh wren by choking out the shrubs and trees where these birds nest.

It is difficult to remove purple loosestrife once it is established, so land managers for wetland areas watch closely for signs of loosestrife invasion, removing any plants that appear. Cut plants must be removed completely and burned or bagged and thrown in a landfill so they cannot resprout.

It is possible to kill purple loosestrife with herbicides, but these chemicals can kill native plants as well, leaving even more bare spots for the loosestrife to move into. Mowing doesn't work well in wetland areas, either. However, grazing sheep can be effective. It was difficult to find insects from loosestrife's native habitat to control the invading population since the plants are not common in their native range. But four have been released so far: two weevils and two leaf-feeding beetles. They appear to be slowing the spread of the plant, reducing it by up to 90 percent in some areas.[13]

GARLIC MUSTARD

Another well-known invasive plant in the eastern United States is garlic mustard. European settlers probably brought this garlicky-smelling plant to the United States for use as food and medicine. It provides an early spring source of vitamins A and C and can be eaten in soups or salads. The seeds can be used to make a spicy mustard.

But despite its usefulness, garlic mustard is a forest nightmare. The plant grows so thickly that it chokes out native wildflowers. It competes for light, water, and nutrients with tree seedlings and inhibits their growth as well. Studies show that garlic mustard puts out chemicals that inhibit mycorrhizal fungi in the soil. These fungi help the roots of tree seedlings capture water and nutrients, so with fewer fungi, the seedlings do not grow as well.

Garlic mustard plants can be boiled with some alum, a powder made from crystals, to create a yellow or green dye.

Few insects or herbivores will eat garlic mustard, so its growth is largely unchecked in areas where it is invasive. Furthermore, it has harmed several native butterflies, including the endangered West Virginia white butterfly, which can't distinguish it from the native

mustard it usually lays eggs on. The caterpillars hatch out normally but cannot survive on the garlic mustard leaves.

Garlic mustard can be removed by hand—very carefully. Cut plants can resprout, so it is important to remove the whole root. The plants should be bagged and thrown in the trash or burned. Burning and herbicides may also be used to control larger patches of garlic mustard.

ROCK SNOT

Its name sounds disgusting, but rock snot is actually a diatom—a single-celled alga also known as didymo. It forms dense, slimy mats in streambeds, choking out organisms that normally live there. This harms the insects and fish that feed on these organisms. Scientists believe rock snot may actually be native to North America. However, it did not become invasive until the past decade, when changing climate conditions allowed it to reproduce in much greater numbers.

Some parks recruit volunteers to pick garlic mustard to slow its spread.

Lionfish feed on many species along coral reefs, including the young of commercially fished species.

Chapter
SIX

FISHY FOES

Colorfully striped lionfish are wreaking havoc on the coral reef ecosystems of the southeastern United States. This invasive fish is native to the South Pacific and Indian Oceans but is rapidly spreading along the Atlantic coast, the Caribbean, and the Gulf of Mexico. Scientists believe the fish were first released into these waters by aquarium owners.

The lionfish is not a picky eater, and it eats a lot. It feeds on small fish, crabs, and shrimp. When lionfish moved in, the biomass of 42 prey species in the Atlantic dropped by 65 percent in just two years.[1] The lionfish hunts by corralling its prey into a corner with its fins and stunning the prey with its venomous spines before chowing down. Its venom can harm humans as well, causing pain, sweating, and swelling.

AQUATIC INVADERS

Lionfish and other aquatic species cause billions of dollars in damage to the environment and to fisheries every year.[2] Some arrive accidentally, usually on boat hulls or in ballast water. Others are released by aquarium owners or intentionally stocked for sportfishing or food. Because many waterways are interconnected, the invaders can quickly spread.

While invasive species can take hold in any body of water, freshwater lakes and ponds seem to be the hardest hit. Like islands, they may be isolated. They also get a lot of traffic because humans use freshwater for so many things, including drinking, transportation, and recreation, such as boating. Because of heavy boat traffic, harvesting of resources, habitat destruction, and pollution, coastal areas are highly susceptible to invasion by exotic species as well.

SPECIES SPOTLIGHT: BLUESPOTTED CORNETFISH

In 1869, a canal connecting the Red Sea to the Mediterranean Sea was opened. Known as the Suez Canal, it quickly became a highway for invasive species. More than 300 species traveled from the Red Sea to the Mediterranean, including fish, worms, crustaceans, and sea slugs.[3] The bluespotted cornetfish, a needlelike fish that preys on other fish, took more than 100 years to make it through the canal. It arrived in the Mediterranean in 2000. From there, it took only two years to reach Italy and eight more to spread to Spain.[4]

CANAL CONNECTIONS

For thousands of years, people have been building canals to connect major waterways. These canals make it easy to carry people and goods far inland or, in the case of the Panama Canal, from one ocean to another. But canals can also serve as channels for invasive species. Some simply swim through the canals to new waterways; others are carried on ships' hulls or in ballast.

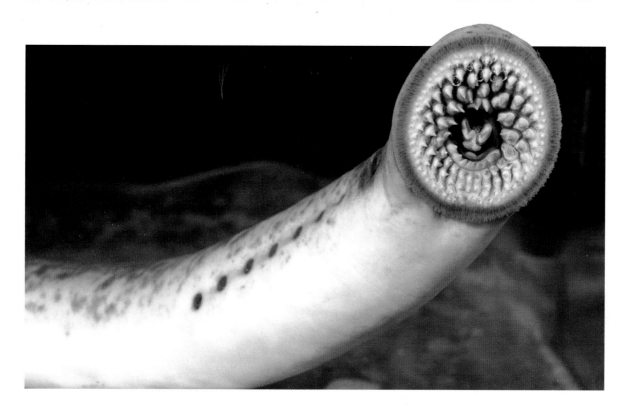

The sea lamprey uses its teeth to grip onto the side of its prey.

The sea lamprey is an example of an invasive species that spread through the man-made Erie Canal. This parasitic fish suctions itself to a larger fish and sucks its blood until the host dies. It reached Lake Ontario before 1830, most likely from the Erie Canal. From there, it spread to the other Great Lakes via canals. Sea lampreys are deadlier than other native lamprey species, and their arrival caused three native fish species to go extinct.[5] They also caused huge economic losses as the harvest of many fish species dropped by at least 90 percent.[6] Electrical and mechanical barriers failed to contain the sea lamprey, but a lampricide, a pesticide that kills only lampreys, has reduced its population in recent years.

SCIENCE CONNECTION
HOW BALLAST WORKS

While it is most efficient for a ship to carry cargo to one port and take on an equal load for its return trip, this does not always happen. Sometimes a ship needs to travel only partially full or empty. When this happens, the ship will float higher in the water and be more prone to tipping over, especially in bad weather. The rudder and propeller will not work as efficiently. When the ship is carrying little or no cargo, water pressure also places more strain on the hull. To compensate, ballast is added. The weight helps to balance the ship and keep it stable in the water.

For thousands of years, ships used heavy materials such as rocks, sand, or roof tiles as ballast. Unfortunately, solid loads of ballast could shift and were difficult and time-consuming to load and unload. So, in the 1880s, ships started using water as ballast instead. Water is easily contained, can be added or removed as needed, and is free. A large tanker can carry more than 7 million cubic feet (200,000 cu m) of ballast water, while a small fishing boat may carry only a few cubic meters.[7]

A ballast pump is used to add or remove water from ballast tanks. The water flows through a sea chest, an opening in the hull below the water level. It passes through several strainers and a sea valve before reaching the tank. However, small organisms can make it through these strainers into the tanks.

One way to prevent organisms from moving from one port to another is to change the water in the ballast tanks mid-ocean. Most species living near the shore cannot survive in the open ocean, and vice versa. Another way is to treat the water in the tanks with electrical pulses, ultraviolet light, heat, sound, magnetic fields, or chemicals. Chemicals must be proven to not harm marine ecosystems. Most systems combine filters and either chlorine or ultraviolet radiation to treat the water.

A ship empties its ballast tank. Small organisms that make it past the filter are released with the water if the ship does not use other treatments.

Sea walnuts' bodies are clear and nearly colorless, but their cilia can refract light into rainbow colors. They are also bioluminescent, giving off a greenish light at night.

INVASION OF THE SEA WALNUTS

It's hard to imagine a more fragile-looking animal than a sea walnut. About the size of golf balls, these clear, delicate comb jellies resemble jellyfish but have no stingers. They feed on tiny animals called zooplankton.

Despite their innocent appearance, sea walnuts managed to crowd out nearly all the fish in Russia's Black Sea in the 1990s. They ate so much that there was little food left for the fish to eat. Sea walnuts were packed into the water so tightly that just 35.3 cubic feet (1 cu m) of water contained thousands of them.[8]

PUTTING A NAME TO THE PROBLEM

English ecologist Charles Elton's 1958 book, *The Ecology of Invasions by Animals and Plants*, was the first to thoroughly examine the issue of invasive species and clearly lay out the problems at hand, even though the term *invasive species* had not yet been coined. Elton wrote about what he called ecological explosions. His book quickly became a scientific classic. For this reason, Elton is sometimes referred to as the father of invasion biology.

Sea walnuts were likely carried from the coast of North and South America to the Black Sea in the ballast of an oil tanker. The polluted waters of the Black Sea provided a perfect environment for their growth, with plenty of food and no natural predators. Sea walnuts can reproduce quickly, releasing up to 8,000 eggs per day.[9] This makes them ideal invaders.

The sea walnut invasion cost tourism and fishing industries in the area more than $350 million.[10] Then, a happy accident turned the tide. Another comb jelly arrived in the Black Sea, likely also carried in ballast water. But this one, called *Beroe*, likes to eat sea walnuts and only sea walnuts. It has reduced the population of sea walnuts in the Black Sea to a manageable level.

However, the battle is not over. Not only do sea walnuts continue to affect the ecosystem, but they have also spread via ships and canals to other nearby seas, including the Caspian, Azov, and Mediterranean, where they are now damaging fisheries.

GREEN CRAB

Small green crabs are munching their way up and down the East and West Coasts of the United States. These European crabs have also invaded coastal waters near South Africa, Australia, Patagonia, and Japan. They likely arrived in ballast water or were used as fish bait.

Green crabs reproduce quickly and in large numbers, and they can tolerate a wide range of water conditions and food sources. Studies show that they are stronger and more aggressive than native crabs, and better at finding food. The crabs like to eat other shellfish, and they also compete with them for food. A single crab can eat 40 small oysters per day. Green crabs devastated the soft-shell clam industry off the East Coast of the United States

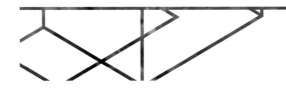

OYSTER KILLER MSX

In 1959, a mysterious oyster killer showed up in Virginia's Mobjack Bay. It killed one million oysters in a single year.[11] Soon it showed up in the Chesapeake and Delaware Bays as well, decimating the oyster populations there. Scientists studying the dead oysters found strange, round cells with multiple nuclei that did not look like any known oyster parasite. They named them Multinucleated Sphere Unknown, or MSX. Scientists still don't know how MSX reproduces or spreads. But they do know that it likely came from Japan or China. Today, MSX can be found in oysters all along the Atlantic Coast, from Florida in the United States to Nova Scotia, Canada. However, the tide may be turning. It appears that some of Maryland's oysters are developing resistance to the parasite. Other populations may eventually follow.

in the 1950s, and some experts are concerned that they may be affecting other shellfish and crabs today.

Between 1999 and 2002, more than 1,100 green crabs were collected from Willapa Bay and Grays Harbor in Washington.[12] But this was not enough to stop their spread. Today, some researchers are studying the possibility of importing a parasitic barnacle that kills green crabs in Europe. Others are exploring ways to turn the small crabs into a profitable food.

ASIAN CARP

The name Asian carp refers to four fish species from Southeast Asia: the bighead, silver, grass, and black carp. These fish were brought to the United States in the 1970s to help control weeds and parasites in ponds and for human consumption. They did a good job of this, but they soon found their way into the Mississippi River. From there, Asian carp have spread into many lakes and rivers in the eastern United States.

Asian carp can grow to more than 100 pounds (45 kg).[13] Some feed on plankton, eating up to 20 percent of their body weight in plankton each day.[14] Others feed on vegetation or mussels and snails. They can damage native plant

AN INVASION HYPOTHESIS

Charles Darwin, best known for his theory of evolution, was one of the earliest scientists to write about invasive species, although he did not use that term. He noticed that exotic plants often replaced native plants and wondered why some species became invasive while others did not. He suggested that species that had faced more competition during their evolution would be able to dominate those that had not, a hypothesis that recent research has confirmed.

Asian carp jump out of the water when startled. Researchers send an electric current through the water to stun the fish so they can be collected.

communities, outcompete native species for food, and lower water quality, which is particularly harmful to filter feeders such as mussels.

Scientists worry that Asian carp may soon reach the Great Lakes and harm the $7 billion fishing industry there.[15] The US Army Corps of Engineers constructed three electric barriers in the Chicago Area Waterway System to prevent carp from entering the Great Lakes. However, carp DNA was recently detected in the Great Lakes, indicating that the fish may have already found their way there.

When startled by boat engines, Asian carp often leap out of the water. Boaters are sometimes injured by these flying fish.

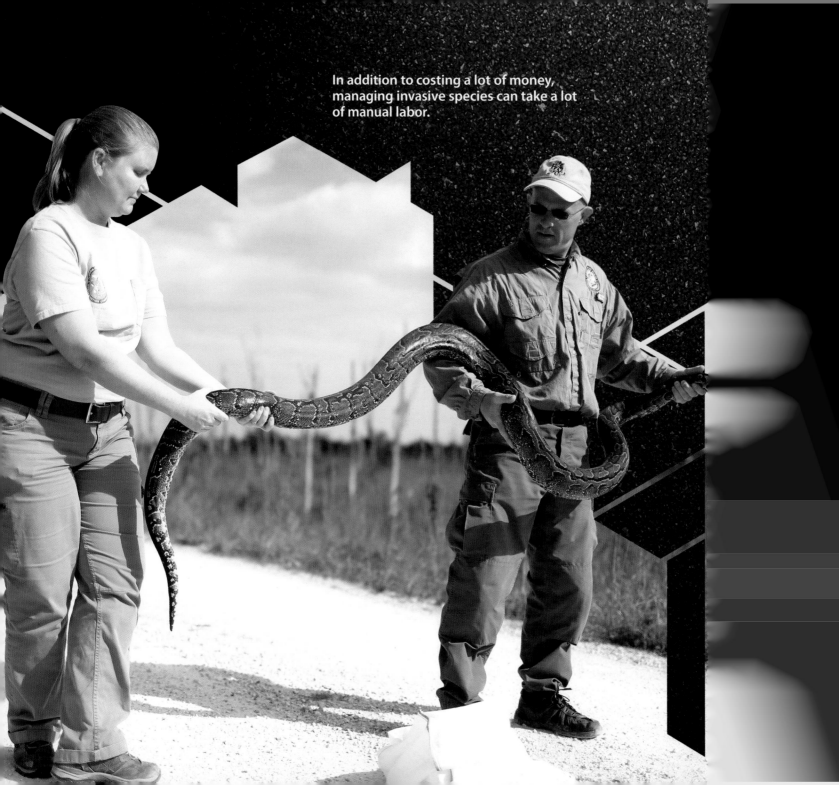

In addition to costing a lot of money, managing invasive species can take a lot of manual labor.

Chapter
SEVEN

COUNTING
THE COSTS

Invasive species often leave paths of destruction behind them. There are environmental costs, such as changes to the environment and damage to native plants or animals, either directly caused by the invaders or as a result of the process of eliminating them. And along with environmental harm, invasive species often come with a huge financial cost to governments, industries, and individuals.

Invasive species cost the United States an estimated $100 to $200 billion per year. Worldwide, losses total approximately $1.4 trillion per year.[1] Some invasive species cause losses by reducing crop and animal harvests. Johnsongrass was planted in the 1800s as animal feed, but sometimes it causes cyanide poisoning in livestock. This weed costs farmers millions of dollars per year in pesticides and reduced crop yields.[2] Norway and black rats cause $19 billion in damages each year by eating stored grain and other products.[3]

SLOW THE SPREAD

The Slow the Spread Program is helping to stop gypsy moths from migrating into new areas. The goal of the program is to put out 100,000 or more traps per year near infested areas.[7] The traps are baited with female pheromones—sex hormones that attract male moths. These traps show when moths are moving into the area and treatment is needed. Possible treatments include *Bacillus thuringiensis* variety *kurstaki*, or Btk, a form of bacterial toxin that kills insects; a virus; pesticides; trapping; and disruption of mating using artificial pheromones. These pheromones are applied to trees to confuse male moths that are searching for females to mate with.

Removing invasive species can also be expensive. For example, both the zebra mussel and Asiatic clam clog water pipes and must be removed by power companies and other industries. In 1989, zebra mussels clogged pipes at a water treatment plant in Monroe, Michigan, leaving the city without drinking water for nearly three days. It cost the city more than $300,000 to clean out the pipes.[4]

The cost of restoring ecosystems and preventing invasions adds up too. From 1999 to 2009, federal and state governments spent $101.2 million to protect and restore wood storks in Florida, where they are threatened by Burmese pythons.[5] In 2010, the federal government spent another $78.5 million trying to keep Asian carp out of the Great Lakes.[6] As invasive species spread, these costs will continue to grow.

THE COST OF CONTAINMENT

On the island of Guam, power outages are normal occurrences. What is not normal about them is their cause: snakes. The brown tree snake arrived on the island from New Guinea in the 1940s, possibly in the cargo hold of a plane or ship. These long, slender snakes slither along power lines, and they frequently short-circuit the cables. They cause nearly 200 power outages per year, costing the island millions of dollars in damages such as food spoilage and computer failure.[8]

As aggravating as this problem is for humans, the snake has caused even bigger problems for native wildlife. The snake feeds on bird and reptile eggs as well as on small animals such as lizards, mice, and birds. It is a good climber and can easily reach nests or sleeping birds in the trees. Guam had no snakes before the brown tree snake's arrival, and the island's birds were defenseless against this type of predator. The birds quickly began to decline. The brown tree snake has wiped out a dozen or more bird species entirely, along with several species of reptiles, bats, and amphibians.[9]

Today, there are approximately two million snakes on the island—as many as 13,000 per square mile (2.6 sq km).[10] This is one of the highest snake densities ever reported. People on

FLYING MICE

In 2013, 2,000 dead mice were airdropped from helicopters into the forests of Guam. They were outfitted with tiny cardboard parachutes and stuffed with acetaminophen, the active ingredient in Tylenol, which is toxic to brown tree snakes. Some of the mice were equipped with tiny radio transmitters to track snake activity. While scientists don't expect this technique to eradicate the snakes, it gives them another weapon in their arsenal.

The brown tree snake can grow up to 9 feet (3 m) in length.[11]

nearby islands are understandably worried that the tree snake will infest their islands as well. The US Department of Agriculture's (USDA's) National Wildlife Research Center estimates that a brown tree snake invasion of Hawaii would cost $1.7 billion per year.[12] The government is making an effort to ensure that it does not happen. The USDA's Animal and Plant Health Inspection Service (APHIS) has more than 60 employees devoted to controlling the brown tree snake.[13] They have a yearly budget of $3 million.[14]

In Guam, more than 8,300 snakes were trapped or poisoned in 2014, especially near the ports.[15] Despite these efforts, snakes occasionally make it into cargo areas. Staff members carefully inspect all vehicles, but the final line of defense comes from a surprising source: dogs. A team of 17 canine super sniffers checks each vehicle before it leaves. The dogs can find snakes that

The USDA uses a dog to check cargo for invasive species. This prevents brown tree snakes from traveling to other places where they may become invasive.

CATCHING A SNAKEHEAD

According to the US Aquatic Nuisance Species Task Force, a group formed to fight nuisance fish and other aquatic invaders, it is important for anglers to learn to identify the northern snakehead. If an angler catches one, he or she should kill it, put it on ice, and take it to the state's DNR, letting the staff know where it was caught.

humans cannot. When they locate a snake, they scratch at the area where it is hidden.

So far, Hawaii has remained free of brown tree snakes. From 1981 to 1998, eight brown tree snakes were found there, alive or dead, all originating from Guam. But the preventive measures put into place since that time appear to be working.

THE COST OF ERADICATION

Snap! Powerful jaws seized the fishhook as soon as it hit the water. The fisherman quickly reeled in his catch. But what on Earth was it? It looked like something from another planet, with spiky teeth and long fins running along the top and bottom of its long, snakelike body. How had this creature come to live in a small pond behind a Maryland shopping center?

It was May 2002. The fisherman threw the strange fish back, but not before taking a photo of his find. When neither he nor his friends could identify it, he checked with the Maryland Department of Natural Resources (DNR). Staff there eventually identified it as a northern snakehead—an invasive species native to China, Russia, and Korea. In Asia, it is considered a delicacy and is grown both as food and to eat pests in rice fields.

The fisherman's strange catch was bad news. This aggressive predator isn't choosy—it eats native fish and competes with them for food. Even worse, snakeheads can breathe air and can survive for up to four days out of water and even longer buried in sediment. Young snakeheads can even travel on land for short distances on their fins. Since the pond was only approximately 75 feet (23 m) from the Little Patuxent River, scientists worried that the fish would spread to other waterways.[16]

The Maryland DNR declared war. It put sandbags around the pond to prevent the snakeheads from escaping over land. It set traps and shot electricity through the water. It sent out anglers galore. Nothing worked. Finally, in August 2002, state biologists killed the remaining fish using chemicals. This was a last-ditch solution, since the pesticide also kills other fish.

The biologists counted more than 1,000 snakeheads among the dead fish. No snakeheads have been found in that pond since. However, a small, unrelated population was later found in the nearby Potomac River, and snakeheads have since been found in several other states.

FREED FISH

The Crofton, Maryland, snakehead invasion was eventually traced to a man who had bought two live snakeheads at an Asian food market. He had planned to make them into a traditional healing soup for his sister, but she recovered in the meantime. When the fish grew too big for his aquarium, he released them into the pond.

Before scientists realized the threat they posed, snakeheads were commonly sold as pets and in live fish markets. Today, they may not be imported or carried across state lines without a permit from the US Fish and Wildlife Service.

COSTS TO HUMAN HEALTH

It's never a good idea to bother a bee, but it's especially dangerous to startle an Africanized honeybee, also called a killer bee. The Africanized honeybee is a cross between two different varieties of honeybee. An African variety was brought to Brazil in 1956 and bred with Italian honeybees to create a hybrid better suited for the tropics. The hybrid

When a honeybee stings a human, it leaves its stinger behind. The honeybee dies, but the stinger can continue pumping venom until it is removed.

bees made less honey and were more aggressive than the Italian bees.

While all honeybees will sting to protect their hives, Africanized bees sting 4 to 10 times more frequently than others, and 10 to 30 times as many of them will fly out to attack an invader.[17] They chase and attack intruders up to 330 feet (100 m) from their hive, twice the distance of regular honeybees.[18] Killer bee venom is no stronger than that of regular honeybees. But the sheer volume of it can seriously injure or kill the bee's victims. Since their arrival in Brazil, the bees have killed approximately 1,000 people and tens of thousands of domestic animals.[19]

The Africanized honeybee continues to take over the hives of European honeybees as it moves northward. Fortunately, the bee is sensitive to cold, so its spread northward will likely be stopped at some point.

ECOSYSTEM COSTS

In 1869, artist and amateur naturalist E. Leopold Trouvelot decided to start a silk business at his Massachusetts home. Regular silkworms didn't grow well in the United States, so he looked for other options. He learned about an insect called the gypsy moth that also made silk cocoons. He brought some gypsy moth egg masses back from France and started raising them on a tree in his backyard. Then, one fateful day, some of them escaped.

The escaped gypsy moths made themselves right at home. They were generalists, feeding on about approximately 600 different species of trees.[20] Within ten years, local outbreaks of the insects had started. By 1890, the Massachusetts government was trying everything possible to get rid of the pests—removing egg masses, spraying chemicals, and even burning forests. But nothing worked. Finally, the government gave up. The gypsy moth spread quickly throughout the Northeast and upper Midwest states, and it continues to spread today. It flies to new areas or lays eggs on the undersides of vehicles, where they are carried away. Gypsy moth eggs can also be carried on hikers' boots.

Female gypsy moths lay their eggs on trees. When the caterpillars hatch, they start chomping leaves. They can destroy all the leaves on a tree, causing it to die within a few years. In some areas, the gypsy moth has killed up to 90 percent of its host trees.[21] The moth has defoliated more than 84 million acres (34 million ha) since 1924.[22]

Gypsy moths can quickly devour a tree's foliage.

EIGHT

FIGHTING
BACK

B efore invasive species can be eliminated, they first need to be identified. But this is not always as easy as it sounds. While newcomers may be easy to spot, others have been around for centuries. Some invasive species can be identified by studying historical documents. Many early European explorers kept notes on the species they observed and even took specimens back to Europe. Some of these can be found

Insect traps can tell researchers if invasive bugs have moved into an area so people can begin to eliminate them.

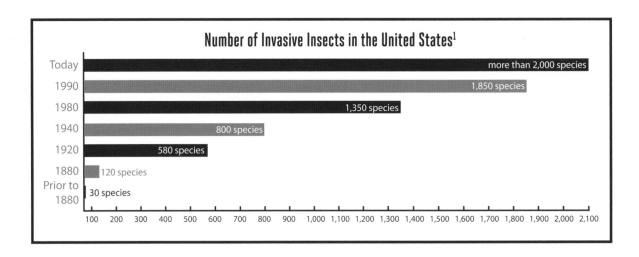

in museums. Otherwise, scientists may need to rely on genetic information and studies on the ecology of a species. They can be identified from the fossil record as well.

It can also be hard to find and identify introduced species before they become widespread. The media, posters, and classes can be used to educate people about invasive species; for example, posters at a lake might remind boaters to clean their boats and empty any ballast water so they don't accidentally transport zebra or quagga mussels. Numerous organizations and agencies have set up hotlines for people to call to report sightings of an invasive species. This helps these organizations to respond quickly to stop the spread of a species before it becomes established.

American bullfrogs are one of the world's 100 worst invasive species.[2] They have invaded the western United States and countries including Japan.

HIGH-TECH TRACKING

Once an invasive species is identified, its spread must be tracked. Scientists are increasingly using technology to help, especially for plants. Satellite images can be used to track

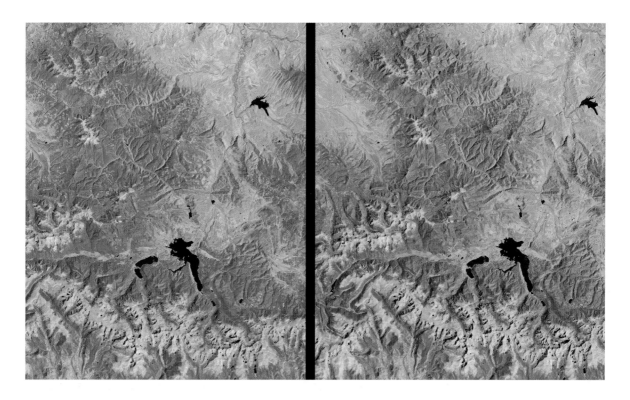

Satellite images can reveal the damage invasive species cause. A Colorado pine forest was much greener before a major pine bark beetle infestation, *left*, than after.

invasions of plants, such as salt cedar and Amur honeysuckle. Smartphone apps and GPS also help scientists track invasive species, often with the help of the public.

Advances in genetics offer new ways of tracking invaders. Next-generation sequencing allows scientists to quickly test an organism's DNA. They can even test DNA left behind in feces and dead skin. This is particularly useful for detecting particles of DNA in water samples. Using this technology, researchers found traces of American bullfrog DNA in Europe even before any bullfrogs had been seen or heard.

Some airports have dogs that sniff out invasive species in people's luggage.

INTEGRATED PEST MANAGEMENT

Once an invasive species has been identified, experts must decide what to do next. A method called integrated pest management (IPM) is often used. This method involves first defining the pest and the threshold at which action should be taken. If the pest reaches the threshold level, actions are taken. These may be cultural, mechanical, biological, or chemical. Generally, a combination of these is most effective. Then the experts evaluate the pest again, correct any issues, and repeat the treatment as needed. Chemicals are used only when needed, and in combination with other methods. The goal is to protect the environment and keep costs low.

CULTURAL METHODS

Cultural control methods aim to keep pests from becoming established, reproducing, surviving, and spreading. They strengthen native species so they can resist invaders. Cultural methods include adding nutrients to soil, seeding native plants to fill in gaps, using detection dogs, and cleaning boats. In a forest, susceptible trees might be removed to limit an outbreak. Controlled fire can keep native plant populations strong and less susceptible to invasive species.

MECHANICAL REMOVAL

One of the simplest ways to control invasive plants is to remove them. However, this is much easier in theory than in practice. It takes a lot of manpower to pull weeds by hand, and the disturbed soil provides a prime place for invasive species to grow back. Mowing works in some cases but is not effective in wet or swampy areas. Special floating harvesters can till or rake plants underwater. However, mowing may harm other nearby plants and animals.

STICK A FORK IN IT!

Chef Chad Wells of Maryland and John Rorapaugh, director of sustainability and sales at a seafood company in Washington, DC, have teamed up to create a novel solution to the snakehead problem: fish dinner! Commercial catfish fishermen often catch snakeheads accidentally in their nets. Rorapaugh buys the snakeheads and supplies them to Wells' restaurant. Customers snap up this tasty invader.

Poisons may kill an invasive species, but they can also harm vulnerable native species.

CHEMICAL SOLUTIONS

Chemical herbicides are often used to control invasive plants such as hydrilla. Their use continues to skyrocket as they are applied to waterways and used on fields, parks, roadsides, and backyards. Chemical pesticides may be used to control invasive animals such as the Asian tiger mosquito or sea lamprey.

These chemicals can help quickly eliminate invasive species by killing many individuals at once. However, they may have serious side effects. Some are known to harm human or animal health. They may also kill other native plants or animals along with the invaders. In addition, herbicide residues can stay in the soil and prevent plants from growing there for a long time. It is important for scientists to weigh the risks with the benefits of various kinds of treatments to determine the best course of action.

BIOLOGICAL CONTROL

Biological control is shortened to biocontrol. There are two types of biocontrol. The classical method involves importing a predator or parasite from the invasive species' native range that feeds only on that species, as *Beroe* eat only sea walnuts. However, careful study is needed to be sure that the new organism will not turn out to be invasive itself. The USDA requires more than five years of testing before approving the release of biological control agents. Potential species must be effective at controlling the target species and must not eat any other species. Once a species is identified, it is tested under strict quarantine before being released into the wild. Even then, this technique doesn't always work—only about one-third of those species introduced have been successful at controlling their target species.

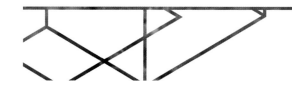

EARTHWORMS
Most people may have never thought of earthworms as an invasive species, but those found in much of Canada and the northern United States are not native to the continent. They were brought to the United States by settlers from Europe, likely in soil carried as ship ballast or in pots of imported plants. Earthworms change forest ecosystems by eating leaf litter, making nutrients easier to access for plants. This makes it easier for invasive plant species to establish themselves, destroying birds' habitat.

Goats have been used to control invasive plant species, such as buckthorn.

The second method of biocontrol is known as augmentation—using natural enemies of a species to control it in a certain area. This includes using goats to mow down kudzu or purchasing parasitic wasps to control whiteflies in a greenhouse. However, many of these species are generalists—they will eat not only the invasive species but others as well—so they must be carefully controlled.

There have been some biocontrol success stories. One of the earliest took place in 1868, when citrus trees in California were devoured by the cottony-cushion scale. This small insect sucks the sap from leaves, twigs, and branches. The USDA Department of Entomology sent a staff member to Australia to research the insect and look for natural predators. He found one: the vedalia ladybird beetle. Five shipments of the beetles were sent to California in 1888 and 1889, and by 1890, the scale had been eliminated. This success paved the way for further biocontrol projects.

The story of the cactus moth does not have such a happy ending. The moth is native to South America, and its larvae feed on cacti. It was set loose in the Caribbean to manage the invasive prickly pear cactus. However, it soon spread to Mexico, Florida, and the southwestern United States. It has seriously damaged the native cacti in these regions. It is critical that

It is important for biocontrol organisms to be host specific. This means that they only eat one specific plant or animal.

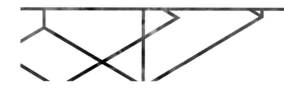

THE MARMORATED STINK BUG

Stink bugs get their name from scent glands on their backs that give off a bad smell if they are threatened or squashed. The brown marmorated stink bug was accidentally brought to Pennsylvania from Asia in the late 1990s. Now it can be found in at least 19 other states and continues to spread.[3] Brown marmorated stink bugs damage farm crops and can become a household pest when cold weather comes and they try to find their way into homes and other buildings.

scientists carefully study a new biocontrol agent before releasing it into the wild to prevent such problems in the future.

LEGAL SOLUTIONS

Numerous laws and treaties have been drafted to try to control the spread of invasive species. In the United States, the Lacey Act of 1900 restricted the entry of fish and wildlife that threaten humans, agriculture, horticulture, forestry, or other wildlife. However, in its early years, this act was rarely enforced. Even today, the act only prohibits species that have been found to cause harm. And by that time, it's too late to prevent damage. It is very difficult to add a species to this list.

Fortunately, however, some agencies can address the issue based on other government directives. With the Plant Quarantine Act of 1912 and the Animal Damage Control Act of 1931, Congress has gradually given government agencies such as APHIS the authority to regulate invasive species.

Many of these laws were updated and consolidated under the 1998 Lacey Act Amendments and 2000 Plant Protection Act. In 1999, the National Invasive Species Council was established. This was part of an executive order signed by President Bill Clinton that requires the government to "provide for restoration of native species and habitat conditions in ecosystems that have been invaded."[4] Approximately one billion dollars per year is set aside to study and control invasive species.[5]

APHIS uses traps to determine how big of a problem invasive insects are in a given area.

The broadest global treaty on invasive species is Article 8(h) of the Convention on Biological Diversity, which was convened in 1992. The article was signed by nearly 200 nations.[6] It states, "Each contracting Party shall, as far as possible and as appropriate, prevent the introduction of, control, or eradicate those alien species which threaten ecosystems, habitats, or species."[7] However, the United States had not ratified the agreement by the end of 2016.

In 2005, the International Maritime Organization set guidelines for managing ship ballast water and sediments. Many countries have created their own regulations as well. However, one issue with these types of regulations is that it is up to each individual country to enforce them. Some are enforced more effectively than others. In a country that borders other nations, it is difficult to keep out invaders if neighboring countries do not share the same commitment to stopping their spread.

Some states have created their own laws about invasive species. In Minnesota, for example, boat owners can be fined if their boats' drain plugs are not removed during transport. Mussel-sniffing dogs are used to search out zebra and quagga mussels, and boaters can be fined $500 if any are found.[8] Florida bans the sale, collection, transport, or cultivation of four

RESTORATION

It's often not enough to simply remove an invasive plant species. The invasive species fills a certain space, or niche, in an ecosystem. Unless it is replaced with native species that originally filled the same niche, the invader may come back—possibly even worse than before. It may take several years to eradicate an invasive species. Planting native species in its place makes the process much more effective.

Minnesota DNR conservation officers inspect boats to make sure they have been drained.

different plant species, including the invasive Melaleuca tree, without a permit from the Department of Environmental Protection.

SUCCESS STORIES

While the devastation caused by invasive species tends to get a lot of press, success stories rarely make the headlines. However, more than 1,000 invasive species have been successfully eradicated worldwide.

Perhaps the most impressive of these stories is the successful removal of nearly 80,000 goats from Santiago Island in the Galápagos island chain. The goats had been introduced by sailors to use as a food source hundreds of years before.[9] While the island was once

Goats ate the same foods as the native Galápagos tortoise, making it harder for the tortoise to find food.

filled with trees, cacti, and wildflowers, the grazers had turned it into a giant grassland. Removing the goats took six years and cost $6 million.[10] Researchers used several methods of tracking the goats, including radio collars and hunting dogs. Some goats were shot from helicopters. By 2009, the goats were gone.

Entomologist Edward F. Knipling of the USDA came up with a creative solution for controlling certain insect pests. Knipling suggested raising males in the laboratory, using radiation to sterilize them, and releasing them into the wild. These sterile males would mate with females so the females could not produce young. This strategy has worked for several pests, including the screwworm in Curaçao in the Caribbean Sea and the melon fly on the island of Rota in the Northern Mariana Islands. A similar method is being studied to fight the Zika virus by releasing genetically modified mosquitoes containing a toxin that will kill their offspring.

Sterile goats fitted with radio collars were set loose on Santiago Island. They led hunters to other goats, which were then eliminated.

Sometimes several methods for removing invasive species are needed, but other times a single, consistent strategy works well. The Asian citrus blackfly only needed one method. It was eliminated from Key West, Florida, when sprayed for three consecutive years with a mixture of oils, soap, and water. Other times, a combination of removal methods is more effective. For example, poisoning and hunting were used to eliminate wild pigs from Santiago Island. When the giant African snail was introduced to Hawaii in 1966, it was eradicated through IPM, using a combination of quarantine, poisoning, and handpicking. In these cases, the combination of methods led to success.

NINE

WHAT CAN WE DO?

Prevention is the most efficient weapon against invasive species. There are simple cultural methods everyone can do to help prevent their spread. The first is to be a responsible pet owner. Never release a pet into the wild. If a pet is no longer wanted, it should be taken to an animal shelter, veterinarian, pet store, or animal rescue organization instead. Aquarium plants or animals should not be dumped

Regularly check that pets' cages are secure. Escaped pets may become invasive.

anywhere they might reach open water, including in the toilet. Pets should be securely contained, and pets should be spayed or neutered when possible to prevent their spread if they do escape.

People can minimize the number of invasive species they transport by following some basic guidelines. Travelers should not bring plants or animals home with them. They should not transport firewood from one area to another, as it may harbor insects or eggs. Boaters should clean boats thoroughly and dump ballast water before moving their boats to a new location. Homeowners should make sure that plants are not invasive before adding them to their landscaping. Hikers should clean their shoes and clothing after hiking to remove seeds and insect eggs. These simple precautions can prevent invasive species from establishing themselves in new areas.

Controlled fires in the Riverlands Migratory Bird Sanctuary in Missouri help prevent invasive species from growing.

WHAT IS CITIZEN SCIENCE?

Citizen science is scientific work performed by members of the general public working together with scientists. Citizen science projects allow scientists to collect much more data at much lower costs than they otherwise could. This concept has been around for a long time. The earliest project was probably the National Audubon Society's Christmas Bird Count, which started on Christmas Day in 1900. But in recent years, citizen-science projects have proliferated as advances in technology have made it easier to share information. Today, there are hundreds of projects that kids and adults can join in the areas of climate change, invasive species, conservation biology, ecological restoration, water quality monitoring, population ecology, and others.

In 2016, 59,039 people in the United States participated in the Christmas Bird Count.

Raising awareness is another important piece of the puzzle. People can write to members of Congress or their local or school newspapers about these issues. They can report any invasive species they see. The USDA's National Invasive Species Information Center website has apps that help identify invasive species. People can also join wildlife groups to help support them in their fight against invasive species, or they can join citizen-science monitoring groups.

CITIZEN SCIENCE

An increasing number of invasive species studies involve the general public in collecting data. These programs are known as citizen science. One successful program in New England includes monitoring by a team of staff and volunteers who are trained to look for invasive plant species. This program, called the Invasive Plant Atlas of New England, is sponsored by the New England Wild Flower Society, the University of Connecticut, the Silvio O. Conte National Fish and Wildlife Refuge, and several government agencies. The volunteers report their findings, which are entered into a database. This data helps scientists determine if a plant species requires management. Another example is EDDMapS, a web-based system run by the Center for Invasive Species and Ecosystem Health at the University of Georgia. Users can submit data on sightings of

Because prevention is the best treatment, early detection and rapid response systems can help prevent, spot, and remove invasive species before they become a problem. Many of these programs rely on citizens to help report and monitor invasions.

HYBRID HOLDS OUT HOPE

In 1904, the fungal disease chestnut blight was carried to the United States on imported plants. It spread quickly through eastern forests, wiping out every chestnut tree in its path. This large, graceful tree that once dominated forests from Georgia to Maine is now nearly extinct.

But science is coming to the rescue. Scientists have created a hybrid tree by breeding the American chestnut with its disease-resistant cousin, the Asian chestnut. The hybrid will be mostly American chestnut, with just enough Asian chestnut to be resistant. Perhaps one day, chestnut trees will again fill the forests of the eastern United States.

invasive plant species along with photos. The data is checked by experts to ensure that the plants are correctly identified.

Kids can get involved in citizen science, too. The Great Lakes Worm Watch offers the opportunity to join an ongoing study or do a private study of earthworms in the Great Lakes area. The Lost Ladybug Project invites kids and adults to find and upload photographs of native ladybugs to help scientists track how they are doing. Participants in the Backyard Bark Beetles project collect bark and ambrosia beetles in traps and mail them to the project headquarters to help researchers track the spread of invasive beetles. These are just a few of the many opportunities for individuals and groups to get involved.

THE BIG PICTURE

One thing that many invasive species have in common is that they like disturbed habitats. A healthy ecosystem has few open ecological niches for new species to take hold. In addition, species are more likely to go extinct if their populations are already low or limited to a small area. This situation may be caused by pollution, overfishing, climate change, or destruction of habitats. By keeping ecosystems healthy, people can minimize the number of species that become invasive. Along with this, stricter laws governing the introduction of new species would dramatically cut down on the number of species entering any given country.

Once invasive organisms have arrived, an early warning system is essential. Educating citizens to recognize such organisms and making it easy for them to report invasive sightings can allow invasive species to be removed quickly, before they become established.

Lastly, once an organism is established, a combination of methods can be used to stop its spread and possibly remove it entirely. These include biocontrol, mechanical removal, chemical use, and genetic warfare. While the problem of invasive species continues to grow, so does humankind's arsenal of knowledge and tools to fight this problem. With the help of technologies such as GPS, genetic testing, and satellite tracking, people may be able to turn the tide in the future.

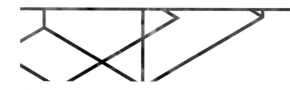

HOW TO REPORT A POTENTIAL INVASIVE SPECIES SIGHTING

If people spot a potentially invasive species in a national or state park, national wildlife refuge, or on other public lands, they can contact the park or refuge office to report it. If it is an aquatic species, they can also report it online at the US Geological Survey's website.

Species lacks resources
and dies

Species is
introduced

Species finds resources
and survives

Competitors and
predators keep the
species in check

Species reproduces

Species becomes
established

Species displaces
native species and
becomes invasive

Species
cannot reproduce

Species dies out

ESSENTIAL FACTS

WHAT IS HAPPENING

Invasive species are organisms that have moved to an ecosystem where they are not native and have caused harm to the plants, animals, or humans already living there.

THE CAUSES

Organisms have always moved around. Some spread naturally; others are carried by human travelers. However, movement is happening at a much higher rate today. People once moved at the speed of a horse or sailing ship. Now they speed around the world in planes, trains, buses, and ships that can cross the ocean in a few days. And they often carry potentially invasive species with them.

WHEN AND WHERE IT'S HAPPENING

Invasive species affect ecosystems worldwide. However, some areas have been harder hit than others. Ecosystems that have been disturbed by human activity are highly susceptible to invasion. Freshwater lakes and rivers, coastal areas, and islands are particularly susceptible as well. More extreme environments, such as deserts and tundras, have suffered fewer effects of invasive species.

KEY PLAYERS

» Humans are both the problem and the solution. They introduce invasive species, both accidentally and on purpose, but they are also working to prevent the species' spread, spot them, and eradicate them.

» Governments are trying to stop species from invading as well as working to control current invasive species. The variety of regulations and enforcement from country to country can make it difficult to prevent invasive species from moving in.

» Scientists are working to find new ways of preventing, identifying, and removing invasive species.

WHAT IT MEANS FOR THE FUTURE

Unless the movement of invasive species is stemmed, they will likely continue to spread, changing and dominating the ecosystems they invade. In some cases, invasive species even change the physical environment, leading to forest fires or landslides. However, new technology offers promising solutions for tracking and eliminating invasive species in the future.

QUOTE

"People are never happy with the species they have."

—*Dr. Daniel Simberloff, ecologist*

GLOSSARY

adapt

To adjust to different conditions.

alien

An organism that evolved somewhere other than its current location.

ballast

Water, rocks, sand, or other heavy material carried aboard a ship to help stabilize it.

biodiversity

The many different plants and animals in an ecosystem.

biomass

An amount of living things in an area.

bounty

A reward offered by the government for capturing or killing an invasive animal and turning it in.

defoliate

To remove leaves from a plant.

ecology

All of the relationships between living things and their environment.

ecosystem

A community of interacting organisms and their environment.

habitat

The natural environment of an organism.

hypothesis

An idea or explanation for something that is subject to scientific investigation.

introduced species

A species living outside its native range that was brought there by humans, either accidentally or on purpose.

invasive species

An organism that arrives in a new ecosystem, takes over, and causes harm.

microbe

A microscopic living thing.

native

A species living in its natural range where it evolved.

nodes

Parts of a plant's stem where leaves grow.

nutrient

A mineral that is absorbed by the roots of plants or digestive systems of animals for nourishment.

organism

A plant, animal, or single-celled life-form.

outcompete

To outdo another organism in a competition for resources.

pest

An animal that bothers or harms humans.

pesticide

A substance or chemical used to destroy pests.

population

A group of organisms of the same species in the same area that could potentially breed with each other.

rhizomes

A plant's horizontal, underground stems that make both shoots above ground and roots.

species

A group of organisms that are very similar and can breed with each other.

territory

The area that an animal defends against others, especially those of the same species.

understory

The bushes and trees below a forest's canopy.

ADDITIONAL RESOURCES

SELECTED BIBLIOGRAPHY

Hamilton, Gary. *Super Species: The Creatures That Will Dominate the Planet*. Buffalo, NY: Firefly Books, 2010. Print.

"Invasive and Exotic Species Profiles." *Invasive.org*. Center for Invasive Species and Ecosystem Health, n.d. Web. 16 Jan. 2017.

Simberloff, Daniel. *Invasive Species: What Everyone Needs to Know*. New York: Oxford UP, 2013. Print.

Simberloff, Daniel, and Marcel Rejmanek. *Encyclopedia of Biological Invasions*. Berkeley, CA: U of California, 2011. Print.

FURTHER READINGS

Aronson, Virginia, and Allyn Szejko. *Iguana Invasion! Exotic Pets Gone Wild in Florida*. Sarasota, FL: Pineapple, 2010. Print.

Barker, David M. *Loss of Biodiversity*. Edina, MN: Abdo, 2011. Print.

Hand, Carol. *Melting Arctic Ice*. Minneapolis, MN: Abdo, 2018. Print.

WEBSITES

To learn more about Ecological Disasters, visit **abdobooklinks.com**. These links are routinely monitored and updated to provide the most current information available.

FOR MORE INFORMATION

For more information on this subject, contact or visit the following organizations:

National Park Service

1849 C Street NW
Washington, DC 20240
202-208-6843
http://nps.gov/

The National Park Service protects the natural and cultural resources of the US National Parks.

The Nature Conservancy

4245 North Fairfax Drive, Suite 100
Arlington, VA 22203-1606
703-841-5300
http://www.nature.org/

The Nature Conservancy works to preserve ecologically important lands and waters around the world.

NOAA's National Ocean Service

N/MB6, SSMC4, Room 9149
1305 East-West Hwy
Silver Spring, MD 20910
301-713-1208
http://oceanservice.noaa.gov/

The National Ocean Service offers solutions to economic, environmental, and social pressures on oceans and coasts.

SOURCE NOTES

CHAPTER 1. A PLAGUE OF . . .

1. "Rabbits—Fact Sheet." *NSW*. Office of Environment and Heritage, 14 Sept. 2015. Web. 23 Feb. 2017.

2. Wendy Zukerman. "Australia's Battle with the Bunny." *ABC Science*. ABC, 8 Apr. 2009. Web. 23 Feb. 2017.

3. Ibid.

4. "In Case of Fire." *The Electric Ben Franklin*. Independence Hall Association, n.d. Web. 16 Feb. 2017.

5. "Economic Impacts." *Invasive.org*. Nature Conservancy, Feb. 2009. Web. 23 Feb. 2017.

6. "Frequently Asked Question about Invasive Species." *Invasive Species*. US Fish and Wildlife Service, 20 Nov. 2012. Web. 23 Feb. 2017.

7. "Global ISU Study: Invasive Species Widespread, but Not More Than at Home Range." *Iowa State University*. Iowa State University of Science and Technology, 1 Mar. 2011. Web. 23 Feb. 2017.

8. "Nile Perch (*Lates Niloticus*)." *Introduced Species Summary Project*. Columbia University, 10 Jan. 2005. Web. 23 Feb. 2017.

9. Sigurdur Greipsson. *Restoration Ecology*. Sudbury, MA: Jones and Bartlett, 2011. Print. 58.

10. Sylvan Ramsey Kaufman and Wallace Kaufman. *Invasive Plants: A Guide to Identification, Impacts, and Control of Common North American Species*. 2nd ed. Mechanicsburg, PA: Stackpole, 2012. Print. 4.

CHAPTER 2. HITCHHIKERS AND ESCAPEES

1. Daniel Simberloff. *Invasive Species: What Everyone Needs to Know*. Oxford: Oxford UP, 2013. Print. 129.

2. "Summary of Public Service, [After 2 September 1800]." *National Archives: Founders Online*. National Historical Publications and Records Commission, 2 Sept. 1800. Web. 23 Feb. 2017.

3. George W. Cox. *Alien Species in North America and Hawaii*. Washington, DC: Island, 1999. Print. 43.

4. "Harlequin Ladybird (*Harmonia axyridis*)." *Wildscreen Arkive*. Wildscreen, n.d. Web. 23 Feb. 2017.

5. "Burmese Python." *National Geographic*. National Geographic, 2017. Web. 23 Feb. 2017.

6. "Invasive Species." *South Florida Ecological Services Field Office*. US Fish and Wildlife Service, 19 Aug. 2016. Web. 23 Feb. 2017.

7. "Invasion of the Giant Pythons: Herpetologist Shawn Heflick Answers Your Questions." *Nature*. WNET, 19 Feb. 2010. Web. 23 Feb. 2017.

8. Darryl Fears. "The Dirty Dozen: 12 of the Most Destructive Invasive Animals in the United States." *Washington Post*. Washington Post, 23 Feb. 2017. Web. 23 Feb. 2017.

9. "Burmese Python." *National Geographic*. National Geographic, 2017. Web. 23 Feb. 2017.

10. "Cats and Other Invasives." *American Bird Conservancy*. American Bird Conservancy, 2017. Web. 23 Feb. 2017.

11. Sigurdur Greipsson. *Restoration Ecology*. Sudbury, MA: Jones and Bartlett, 2011. Print. 151.

12. *Invasive Plants and Forest Ecosystems*. Ed. Ravinder Kumar Kohli, et al. Boca Raton, FL: CRC, 2009. Print. 416.

13. "Zebra Mussel (*Dreissena Polymorpha*)." *MN Department of Natural Resources*. Minnesota DNR, 2017. Web. 23 Feb. 2017.

14. Souyad Boudjelas, et al. "100 of the World's Worst Invasive Alien Species: A Selection from the Global Invasive Species Database." Auckland, NZ: ISSG, 2000. *IUCN*. Web. 23 Feb. 2017.

15. David Armitage. "*Rattus Norvegicus*: Brown Rat." *Animal Diversity Web*. University of Michigan, 2004. Web. 23 Feb. 2017.

16. "*Dreissena polymorpha*." *NAS – Nonindigenous Aquatic Species*. USGS, 26 Jan. 2017. Web. 24 Feb. 2017.

CHAPTER 3. FUEL TO THE FIRE

1. "Future of Climate Change." *EPA*. US Environmental Protection Agency, 27 Dec. 2016. Web. 23 Feb. 2017.

2. "Hawaii Is 'The Endangered Species Capital of the World.'" *Huffington Post*. Huffington Post, 1 Dec. 2015. Web. 23 Feb. 2017.

3. Tao Orion. *Beyond the War on Invasive Species: A Permaculture Approach to Ecosystem Restoration*. White River Junction, VT: Chelsea Green, 2015. Print. 99.

4. Daniel Simberloff. *Invasive Species: What Everyone Needs to Know*. Oxford: Oxford UP, 2013. Print. 41.

5. "Cane Toads Leap Across Australia." *National Geographic*. National Geographic, 28 Sept. 2016. Web. 23 Feb. 2017.

6. "Cane Toad." *Queensland Museum*. Queensland Museum, 2017. Web. 23 Feb. 2017.

7. John R. Platt. "Frog Mass Extinction on the Horizon." *Scientific American*. Scientific American, 13 Oct. 2015. Web. 23 Feb. 2017.

CHAPTER 4. INVASIVE LAND ANIMALS

1. Sigurdur Greipsson. *Restoration Ecology*. Sudbury, MA: Jones and Bartlett, 2011. Print. 154.

2. "European Starling." *All about Birds*. Cornell University, 2015. Web. 23 Feb. 2017.

3. George M. Linz, et al. "European Starlings: A Review of an Invasive Species with Far-Reaching Impacts." *Managing Vertebrate Invasive Species: Proceedings of an International Symposium*. Digital Commons at University of Nebraska–Lincoln, Aug. 2007. Web. 23 Feb. 2017.

4. Andrea Alfano. "How Do Starling Flocks Create Those Mesmerizing Murmurations?" *All about Birds*. Cornell University, 21 Feb. 2013. Web. 23 Feb. 2017.

5. Jon Mooallem. "Pigeon Wars." *New York Times*. New York Times, 15 Oct. 2006. Web. 23 Feb. 2017.

6. Tao Orion. *Beyond the War on Invasive Species: A Permaculture Approach to Ecosystem Restoration*. White River Junction, VT: Chelsea Green, 2015. Print. 16.

7. "European Starling." *All about Birds*. Cornell University, 2015. Web. 23 Feb. 2017.

8. "Nutria, an Invasive Rodent." *Wildlife Services*. APHIS, Oct. 2010. Web. 23 Feb. 2017.

9. Darryl Fears. "The Dirty Dozen: 12 of the Most Destructive Invasive Animals in the United States." *Washington Post*. Washington Post, 23 Feb. 2015. Web. 23 Feb. 2017.

10. "Louisiana Coastwide Nutria Control Program." *Nutria*. Louisiana Department of Wildlife and Fisheries, 2007. Web. 23 Feb. 2017.

11. Ibid.

12. "In the News: South Georgia to Cull Invasive Reindeer." *Arkive Blog*. Wildscreen, 10 Jan. 2013. Web. 23 Feb. 2017.

13. "Pest Fact Sheet: Giant African Snail." *Asia-Pacific Forest Invasive Species Network*. FAO, n.d. Web. 23 Feb. 2017.

14. "Nine-Banded Armadillo: *Dasypus Novemcinctus*." *BioKids*. University of Michigan, 2017. Web. 23 Feb. 2017.

15. Rebecca G. Harvey and Frank J. Mazzotti. The Argentine Black and White Tegu in South Florida: Population Growth, Spread, and Containment." *EDIS*. University of Florida, 2015. Web. 23 Feb. 2017.

CHAPTER 5. HOW PLANTS MOVE AROUND

1. "Kudzu." *Forest Invasive Plants Resource Center*. USDA Forest Service, n.d. Web. 23 Feb. 2017.

2. Sigurdur Greipsson. *Restoration Ecology*. Sudbury, MA: Jones and Bartlett, 2011. Print. 165.

3. Susan L. Woodward and Joyce A. Quinn. *Encyclopedia of Invasive Species: From Africanized Honey Bees to Zebra Mussels*. Santa Barbara, CA: Greenwood, 2011. Print. 1: 623.

4. "Kudzu." *Washington Invasive Species Council*. Recreation and Conservation Office, 2009. Web. 23 Feb. 2017.

5. Richard J. Blaustein. "Kudzu's Invasion into Southern United States Life and Culture." *US Forest Service Southern Research Station.* USDA, 2001. Web. 23 Feb. 2017.

6. Sharon Dowdy. "Kudzu Vine Key to Kudzu Bug's Survival." *College of Agriculture and Environmental Sciences.* University of Georgia, 28 June 2012. Web. 23 Feb. 2017.

7. "Kudzu (*Pueraria Montana*)." *New York Invasive Species Network.* Cornell University, 2017. Web. 23 Feb. 2017.

8. Sigurdur Greipsson. *Restoration Ecology.* Sudbury, MA: Jones and Bartlett, 2011. Print. 169.

9. Stevan Z. Knezevic. "EC03-177 Noxious Weeds of Nebraska: Purple Loosestrife." *Historical Materials from University of Nebraska–Lincoln Extension.* 2003. *ResearchGate.* Web. 23 Feb. 2017.

10. "White-Nose Syndrome: Questions and Answers." *Center for Biological Diversity.* Center for Biological Diversity, n.d. Web. 1 Mar. 2017.

11. Susan L. Woodward and Joyce A. Quinn. *Encyclopedia of Invasive Species: From Africanized Honey Bees to Zebra Mussels.* Santa Barbara, CA: Greenwood, 2011. Print. 1: 415.

12. Daniel Simberloff. *Invasive Species: What Everyone Needs to Know.* Oxford: Oxford UP, 2013. Print. 55.

13. "Biological Control of Purple Loosestrife." *MN Department of Natural Resources.* Minnesota DNR, 2017. Web. 23 Feb. 2017.

CHAPTER 6. FISHY FOES

1. Stephanie J. Green, et al. "Invasive Lionfish Drive Atlantic Coral Reef Fish Declines." *PLOS One* 7.3 (7 Mar. 2012): e32596. *US National Library of Medicine National Institutes of Health.* Web. 23 Feb. 2017.

2. "What Are Aquatic Invasive Species?" *Fish and Aquatic Conservation.* US Fish and Wildlife Service, 2 Nov. 2015. Web. 23 Feb. 2017.

3. Peter T. Harris and Elaine K. Baker. *Seafloor Geomorphology as Benthic Habitat: GeoHAB Atlas of Seafloor Geomorphic Features and Benthic Habitats.* 1st ed. Boston, MA: Elsevier, 2012. Print. 50.

4. Daniel Simberloff. *Invasive Species: What Everyone Needs to Know.* Oxford: Oxford UP, 2013. Print. 52.

5. Ibid. 37.

6. Ibid. 64.

7. *Stemming the Tide: Controlling Introductions of Nonindigenous Species by Ships' Ballast Water.* Washington, DC: National Academy, 1996. *National Academies Press.* Web. 23 Feb. 2017.

8. "Jellyfish Gone Wild: Locations: Black Sea." *National Science Foundation.* National Science Foundation, n.d. Web. 23 Feb. 2017.

9. Ibid.

10. Ibid.

11. Jack Greer. "Killer from across the Sea." *Chesapeake Quarterly.* Maryland Sea Grant, June 2009. Web. 23 Feb. 2017.

12. "*Carcinus Maenas* (European Green Crab)." *Conservation: Aquatic Invasive Species.* Washington Department of Fish and Wildlife, 2017. Web. 23 Feb. 2017.

13. "Asian Carp Overview." *Mississippi National River and Recreation Area Minnesota.* National Park Service, n.d. Web. 23 Feb. 2017.

14. Ibid.

15. Ibid.

CHAPTER 7. COUNTING THE COSTS

1. Sigurdur Greipsson. *Restoration Ecology.* Sudbury, MA: Jones and Bartlett, 2011. Print. 151.

2. Jeannette E. Warnert. "Invasive Superweed Johnsongrass Is the Target of a New Nationwide Research Effort." *Green Blog.* University of California, 4 Mar. 2016. Web. 23 Feb. 2017.

3. "The Cost of Invasive Species." *US Fish and Wildlife Service.* US Fish and Wildlife Service, Jan. 2012. Web. 23 Feb. 2017.

4. William Rapai. *Lake Invaders: Invasive Species and the Battle for the Future of the Great Lakes*. Detroit: Wayne State University, 2016. Print. 4.

5. "The Cost of Invasive Species." *US Fish and Wildlife Service*. US Fish and Wildlife Service, Jan. 2012. Web. 23 Feb. 2017.

6. Ibid.

7. "'Slow the Spread': A National Program to Contain the Gypsy Moth." *US Forest Service: Northern Research Station*. US Department of Agriculture, Apr. 2007. Web. 23 Feb. 2017.

8. "Brown Tree Snake." *Hawaii Invasive Species Council*. State of Hawaii, 2017. Web. 23 Feb. 2017.

9. Ibid.

10. M. Alex Johnson. "Two Thousand Mice Dropped on Guam by Parachute—to Kill Snakes." *NBC News*. NBC News, 2 Dec. 2013. Web. 23 Feb. 2017.

11. "Brown Tree Snake." *Hawaii Invasive Species Council*. State of Hawaii, 2017. Web. 23 Feb. 2017.

12. Ibid.

13. "Brown Tree Snake an Invasive Reptile." *Wildlife Services*. APHIS, Jan. 2011. Web. 23 Feb. 2017.

14. "H. Rept. 108-687—BROWN TREE SNAKE CONTROL AND ERADICATION ACT OF 2004." *Congress.gov*. US Congress, 2004. Web. 23 Feb. 2017.

15. Senior Airman Katrina M. Brisbin. "USDA Dogs Sniff Out Snakes." *Air Reserve Personnel Center*. US Air Force, 5 May 2015. Web. 23 Feb. 2017.

16. Hillary Mayell. "Maryland Wages War on Invasive Walking Fish." *National Geographic News*. National Geographic, 2 July 2002. Web. 23 Feb. 2017.

17. Phillip Moore, et al. "Africanized Bees: Better Understanding, Better Prepared." *Extension*. Extension, 19 Aug. 2015. Web. 23 Feb. 2017.

18. Ibid.

19. Ibid.

20. R. Chris Williamson. "Gypsy Moth." *Wisconsin Horticulture*. University of Wisconsin, 13 Aug. 2012. Web. 23 Feb. 2017.

21. Daniel Simberloff. *Invasive Species: What Everyone Needs to Know*. Oxford: Oxford UP, 2013. Print. 69.

22. "'Slow the Spread': A National Program to Contain the Gypsy Moth." *US Forest Service: Northern Research Station*. US Department of Agriculture, Apr. 2007. Web. 23 Feb. 2017.

CHAPTER 8. FIGHTING BACK

1. Daniel Simberloff. *Invasive Species: What Everyone Needs to Know*. Oxford: Oxford UP, 2013. Print. 39–40.

2. "American Bullfrog (*Lithobates catesbeianus*)." *Wildscreen Arkive*. Wildscreen, n.d. Web. 23 Feb. 2017.

3. "Brown Marmorated Stink Bug." *Insect Advice from Extension*. PennState College of Agriculture Sciences, 2017. Web. 23 Feb. 2017.

4. "Executive Order 13112 of February 3, 1999." *Government Publishing Office*. GPO, 3 Feb. 1999. Web. 23 Feb. 2017.

5. Tao Orion. *Beyond the War on Invasive Species: A Permaculture Approach to Ecosystem Restoration*. White River Junction, VT: Chelsea Green, 2015. Print. 17.

6. "The CBD and Invasive Alien Species." *Convention on Biological Diversity*. UN Environment, 2009. Web. 23 Feb. 2017.

7. Ibid.

8. "Minnesota Invasive Species Laws." *MN Department of Natural Resources*. Minnesota DNR, 2017. Web. 23 Feb. 2017.

9. Virginia Hughes. "Galápagos Week: When Conservation Means Killing." *Phenomena: A Science Salon*. National Geographic, 9 Aug. 2013. Web. 23 Feb. 2017.

10. Ibid.

CHAPTER 9. WHAT CAN WE DO?

None

INDEX

ABOUT THE AUTHOR

Lisa J. Amstutz is the author of more than 50 children's books. Her work has also appeared in a wide variety of magazines and newspapers. A former outdoor educator, Amstutz specializes in topics related to science, nature, and agriculture. Her background includes a BA in biology from Goshen College and an MS in environmental science/ecology from the University of Virginia. Amstutz lives with her family on a hobby farm in rural Ohio.